GOD ON TRIAL

THE BOOK OF JOB
AND
HUMAN SUFFERING

Bill Thomason

A Liturgical Press Book

THE LITURGICAL PRESS
Collegeville, Minnesota

1	2	3	4	5	6	7	8

Library of Congress Cataloging-in-Publication Data

Thomason, Bill, 1943–
    God on trial : the book of Job and human suffering / Bill Thomason.
      p. cm.
    Includes bibliographical references.
    ISBN 0-8146-2424-3
    1. Bible. O.T. Job—Criticism, interpretation, etc. 2. Job (Biblical figure)
    3. Suffering—Religious aspects—Christianity.
    I. Title.
    BS1415.2.T47   1997
    233'.106—dc20   96-32842
                                                      CIP

To
Dr. Gregory Pritchard,
who taught me it is all right
to ask questions

The courage to be is the ethical act in which man affirms his own being in spite of those elements of his existence which conflict with his essential self-affirmation.

—Paul Tillich, *The Courage To Be*

Contents

Preface

I first taught the Book of Job in the mid-1970s to an adult education class at Crescent Hill Baptist Church in Louisville, Kentucky. As I prepared for those sessions, I was surprised to find that the person of Job in the biblical book is the antithesis of the Job I had always heard about. This new, unfamiliar Job is not patient, long-suffering, and accepting of every evil that happens to him. Instead, he is impatient, short to suffer (especially foolish attempts to explain his plight by the traditional way of Wisdom), and utterly unwilling to accept what had befallen him.

He is also intellectually curious and capable of exploring the ramifications of his suffering—two traits noticeably missing in the three friends who come to "comfort" him. Job is, in short, a very attractive person, a model of human integrity holding steady in almost impossible circumstances.

This is a Job we all need to know, and I commend him to you.

I want to acknowledge my gratitude to the following people: Pete Dwyer, Kay Weiss, Mark Twomey, and Colleen Stiller of The Liturgical Press for their support of this work; Janet Hoomes, once again, for her excellent work in preparing the manuscript for the publisher; and my wife, Bobbie, for her unfailing support and (in contrast to Job) her unflagging patience as I worked and reworked the manuscript.

This book is dedicated to Dr. Gregory Pritchard, who introduced me to philosophy when I was a sophomore at Oklahoma Baptist University. Dr. Pritchard, like Job, knew how to ask the right questions.

Chapter 1

The Book of Job
and Our Misconceptions

"Ye have heard of the patience of Job," James 5:11 declares; and, of course, we *have* heard of Job's patience. In fact, we cannot think *Job* without also thinking *patience.* Job has become the model for long-suffering endurance in the face of severe provocation. Parents invoke Job's patience when disciplining recalcitrant children. Teachers invoke Job's patience when counseling problem students. Wives and husbands invoke Job's patience when suffering wayward spouses.

The Problem with Job's "Patience"

Where did we get this notion that Job was patient? Surely it must come from the Book of Job itself where we read of a prosperous yet pious man who loses everything, refuses to blame God, and patiently accepts his fate: "The Lord gives and the Lord takes away; blessed be the name of the Lord." "Throughout all this," the ancient storyteller concludes, "Job did not utter one sinful word" (1:21-22).

Job, therefore, becomes a model. We ought to be like Job. When suffering comes, we ought to be patient and submissive, waiting for God to make everything right. We ought to accept our fate without questioning. It is God's will, our counselors say, trying to comfort us. To question, to feel anger, bitterness, or frustration is sinful. We ought to be like Job, we are told, who did not "utter one sinful word."

This is the popular image of Job, this is the Job-we-all-know. Most of us, though, are uneasy with this Job. Deep down inside we don't like this stoic figure. We think to ourselves (hoping no one can read our thoughts), if those things happened to me, God would have a lot of explaining to do. Consequently, we feel guilty. Beneath the surface of our public selves is the private recognition that we could never be patient and accepting like this Job. We know we would feel rebellious. But (we think) we are supposed to be like this Job. And so, an internal conflict begins between what we think we ought to be and what we know we honestly are. This Job-we-all-know is, in the last analysis, a discouraging figure.

But to say that we can't be like this Job is really to say that we don't *want* to be like him. In the face of meaningless suffering our deepest, most human response is a desire to do something about it, at least to find an explanation for it. But Job (we believe) did not react this way. He simply accepted his suffering as coming from God. So, we conclude, we either must be rebels, cut off from God, or we must give up our deepest moral intuitions. We feel forced to choose between God and our integrity.

The foregoing should give us pause. The Book of Job, after all, is supposed to be one of the great works of literature. Yet, this image of the Job-we-all-know (which is found in the prologue and epilogue of the Book of Job) is hardly great literature. It is a fine story, artfully told. But its characters are mere puppets manipulated by cosmic forces about which they know nothing and over which they have no control. This story lacks universality and depth of insight. Is there, perhaps, something we are overlooking?

To answer this question we must read the book in such a way that our misconceptions are minimized. We should, first of all, read it in a modern translation. The familiar and beloved King James Version of 1611 is often a translation from one obscurity (a notoriously difficult and problematic Hebrew text) to another (the beautiful but archaic English of post-Elizabethan times). Furthermore, we need a translation which clearly distinguishes the poetic dialogue (Job 3:1–42:6) from the prose prologue (Job

1–2) and epilogue (Job 42:7-17).[1] We also need to free ourselves as much as possible from preconceptions and read what the protagonist, Job, actually *says*, beginning in chapter 3. We need to be on guard against the red herrings of the prologue and epilogue: Why does God bargain with Satan? Is Satan the devil of traditional Christian theology? Why did Job have twice as much material wealth at the end but only the same number of sons and daughters? The primary function of the prologue, like that of any good story, is to hook us, to get our attention, to rouse our curiosity. The function of the epilogue is to tie up the loose ends of the traditional story. Speculation about the wager between God and Satan or Job's material assets at the end of the story attributes theological significance to literary devices, whose functions are to introduce and close the drama of Job's suffering.

To further our understanding, we need to consider the following matters: the nature of the book, its organization, its content, and its purpose.

Job and Wisdom Literature

The Book of Job begins as a morality tale whose theme is disinterested religion. As Satan says to God in chapter 1, "Has not Job good reason to be godfearing?" Or, as the King James Version has it, "Doth Job fear God for nought?" We are, therefore, set up for a story about how a typical near eastern sage would deal with a challenge to his religion. We are prepared to expect a subtle dialogue cleverly defending the accepted wisdom of the day. Job is, in other words, usually considered an example of wisdom literature (which includes Proverbs, Ecclesiastes, and some of the Psalms as well).

---

1. The following English translations distinguish prose from poetry: *The New Revised Standard Version* (NRSV, the text cited in this book); *The New American Bible* (NAB); *The New Jerusalem Bible* (NJB); *The Good News Bible* or *Today's English Version* (TEV); *The New International Version* (NIV); and the *Revised English Bible* (REB, in some ways the most readable translation). *The King James Version* (KJV) ought to be read in conjunction with these others—the KJV for the beauty of its language, the others for understanding.

In some ways such literature is not typical of the Hebrew Bible, whose more characteristic expression is the Law and the Prophets. The Law and Prophets are based on divine revelation. Moses ascends Mt. Sinai, and God gives him the Ten Commandments. The prophets hear and proclaim "the Word of the Lord." Wisdom literature, in contrast, generally draws on the common fund of human experience rather than appealing to divine revelation. The sages of the ancient Near East taught that one should refrain from sin (adultery, say, or dishonesty in business), not primarily because the Law forbids it or a prophet rails against it, but rather because human experience shows that such behavior usually turns out bad in the end. The appeal in Wisdom literature is to prudence, to pragmatic calculation of the consequences of action. Experience is the guide because it provides the evidence that certain kinds of behavior lead to certain kinds of consequences. Job is an example of Wisdom literature in that Job's friends counsel him in terms of the accumulated fund of current wisdom.

In some important ways, however, Job is not at all like Wisdom literature. For one thing, Job challenges the accepted wisdom of his day by citing his experience against that of his friends. When experience contradicts experience, what will the sage do? In the Book of Job, this contradiction is resolved finally through divine revelation—God appears at the end and has the final word. For another thing, the morality play of the first two chapters—so typical an expression of Wisdom ethos—quickly gives way in chapter 3 to an unsettling dialogue on why innocent people like Job suffer, the real focus of the book. Since the author rejects the traditional Wisdom answer and offers no new solution, we are cut loose from our usual moral moorings and find ourselves adrift in uncharted ethical and theological waters, not sure which way to steer. The function of Wisdom literature is to anchor its readers in the fundamental precepts of action—which, if followed, will guarantee a long and happy life. The Book of Job signally disregards this primary function and in fact has the opposite effect. Again, we are led away from construing Job as Wisdom literature.

The truth is that the Book of Job, taken as a whole, is unlike anything else ever written. It is *sui generis*. It is a poem, to be sure, but it is unlike any other poem. It is not an epic, though it deals with an epic theme. It is not a lyric, though (even in translation) there are passages of lyric beauty. It is not a drama, though it is dramatic. The Book of Job is simply the Book of Job, and there is nothing else quite like it in all of world literature.

Organization of the Book of Job

The Book of Job is carefully organized. The poetry is set in a prose framework and divided into three cycles of speeches by Job and his friends, followed by Job's summary of his case, and then by the speeches of Elihu and God. The following is one possible outline of the book (parentheses indicate chapter divisions):

Prose Prologue (1–2)
Job's Curse (3)
The First Cycle of Speeches (4–14)
  Eliphaz's Speech (4–5)
  Job's Response (6–7)
  Bildad's Speech (8)
  Job's Response (9–10)
  Zophar's Speech (11)
  Job's Response (12–14)
The Second Cycle of Speeches (15–21)
  Eliphaz's Speech (15)
  Job's Response (16–17)
  Bildad's Speech (18)
  Job's Response (19)
  Zophar's Speech (20)
  Job's Response (21)
The Third Cycle of Speeches (22–27, 28?)
  Eliphaz's Speech (22)
  Job's Response (23–24)
  Bildad's Speech (25; only six verses total)
  Job's Response (26–27)
  [No speech by Zophar or response by Job]
  A Hymn to Wisdom (28; attributed to Job)
Job's Final Survey of His Case (29–31)
  His Past Good Fortune (29)
  His Present Plight (30)

His Oath of Clearance (31)
Elihu's Speeches (32–37)
    Elihu's Self-Introduction (32)
    God's Sovereignty (33–36:23)
    The Majestic God of the Storm (36:24–37:24)
God's First Speech (38:1–39:30; 41:1-6)
    God's Sovereignty Over the Physical World (38:1–39:30; 41:1-6)
    God's Address to Job and Job's Response (40:1-5)
God's Second Speech (40:6-24; 41:7-34)
    God's Justice in Human Affairs (40:6-14)
    The Crocodile (40:15-24; 41:7-34)
    God's Second Address to Job and Job's Submission (42:1-6)
The Prose Epilogue (42:7-17)

This outline draws our attention immediately to the fundamental character of the poetry as a series of set speeches with a highly formalized, artificial structure. Job 3–31 seems to form a unity with the repeated pattern of Eliphaz-Job, Bildad-Job, Zophar-Job. The bracketing of these speeches by two of Job's—the curse of chapter three and his final defense in chapters 29–31—reinforces their unity. But clearly the pattern breaks down in the third cycle, where Bildad's speech is only five verses in length (the friends' speeches average twenty-nine verses up to this point) and Zophar's speech, with Job's response, is missing. Is this breakdown deliberate on the poet's part, or has something happened to disrupt the third cycle? This outline provides one clue—the hymn to Wisdom attributed to Job. This hymn is a beautiful, meditative psalm expressing wonder at the mystery of Wisdom. But it breathes the calm air of the sage's study rather than the poisonous atmosphere of the rubbish heap where the dialogue has thus far been conducted. In other words, chapter 28 seems out of place and therefore indicates some sort of alteration to the original text. Job's final response to his friends in chapters 26–27 confirms this impression, because in these chapters Job says things that contradict his earlier, adamantly held positions. Job sounds more like one of his friends than he does himself.

    Another set of questions arise because of Elihu's speeches. Elihu is not mentioned before chapter 32, and once he finishes speaking he is not mentioned again. His speeches comprise the longest continuous statement by any of the characters. They are only broken by an occasional "Then Elihu went on to say." Contrary to what we would expect, Job does not respond to Elihu, though Elihu repeats many of the three friends' arguments against Job. On the face of it, it seems that Elihu's speeches were not an original part of the poem. Otherwise he would have been mentioned along with the other friends and included in the dialogue throughout. Furthermore, by the end of chapter thirty-one we are prepared for God to appear. Instead, we have Elihu, a pompous, bombastic, and intense youth. Who, then, wrote these speeches— the original poet or someone else? Why were they written and inserted at this point? How do they relate to the rest of the poem?

God's speeches raise a third set of questions. The first speech has apparently been disrupted, its last six verses having been transposed to the beginning of chapter 41.[2] And the second speech, with its powerful description of the crocodile, appears to be largely irrelevant to the questions Job has asked. Is the disruption in the first speech deliberate or accidental? Did the original poet write the poem on the crocodile, and was it original to the text or added later?

We cannot answer these questions at this point, but we can draw some general conclusions about the original text of the poem. The original poem probably consisted of Job's curse, the three cycles of speeches (with the third cycle intact), Job's summary of his case, and God's speeches from the storm. Outlined, the original poem would have looked like this:

> Job's Curse (3)
> The First Cycle of Speeches (4–14)
> The Second Cycle of Speeches (15–21)
> The Third Cycle of Speeches (22–27; plus material now missing)
> Job's Final Summary of His Case (29–31)
> God's Speeches (38:1–42:6)

In the transmission of the text, the Hymn to Wisdom (chapter 28) and Elihu's speeches were added, and the third cycle of speeches and God's first speech suffered disruption. The speech on the

---

2. Here I am following the order of the REB.

crocodile may also be a later addition. These problems should caution us to take care in interpreting Job. We do not have the text now as it was originally written.

Content and Purpose

The Book of Job begins with an artful retelling of an old legend familiar throughout the near east. In this legend Job is immensely wealthy, immensely pious, and immensely respected. He loses everything that makes life worth living yet refuses to blame God. Instead, he patiently resigns himself to his fate with the consolation that God gives or takes away as God pleases. God, who has wagered with Satan over Job's fidelity, wins the bet and rewards Job with a twofold increase in material assets and another set of seven sons and three daughters. Job also regains his lost status in the community and lives to "a very great age." Job is the wise one who deals wisely with adversity—patient acceptance, faithfulness to God—assured that in the end everything will be right. The prologue and epilogue put Job on trial, and he is found innocent.

In the poetry, however, which constitutes the bulk of the book, we discover a second, very different Job. In this second version, Job is still a good man who loses everything that makes living worthwhile. But in this version, Job almost loses his religion as well. His whole world has crumbled, and instead of being patient and submissive, he demands an explanation. He believes he has a right to an explanation because it is *his* life that has been ruined. If God will not give him the explanation he desires, then he will be forced to conclude that God is not really just after all. In the poetry, Job puts *God* on trial. His friends, who have heard about his distress and have come to console him, are horrified at his disfigured countenance *and* his unorthodox, shocking, dangerous questions. Job is flirting with blasphemy, and the friends see it as their duty to discourage this romance. The only way they know to do this is to assume that Job is guilty of something and to make him to admit his guilt; because if Job has not sinned, then God *does* seem to be unjust as Job has charged. Implicitly at first, then explicitly with growing anger toward Job, they argue that he deserves the suffering visited upon him. Job responds by defending his integrity and accusing his friends of faithlessness. He rejects in no uncertain terms their explanation that suffering always results from sin, but he is unable to discover a better one. Instead, Job does explore the ways he might get satisfaction—either a third party could arbitrate, or God could appear and Job could question God. Job finally silences his friends with a summary of his defense, ending with a mighty oath of clearance. He too falls silent and awaits God's response.

This response is delayed, however, by the longest continuous series of speeches, those of the pompous, bombastic, and earnest youth Elihu, who repeats many of the friends' arguments but who also contributes two new elements. The first is the idea of suffering being a signal from a gracious God to turn the sinner from sin, instead of being merely punishment. The second is a magnificent, thrilling description of the thunderstorm, which introduces, finally, the speeches of God. The divine speeches out of the thunderstorm consist of overwhelming rhetorical questions which have the effect of silencing Job. Job had demanded God's appearance so he could question God. But when God does appear, God does the questioning, not Job. Job the rebel "melts away" and his questions no longer seem relevant in the light of his encounter with the living God. Curiously, though, God vindicates Job because when the speeches are ended, God says to Eliphaz: "My anger is aroused against you and your two friends, because, unlike my servant Job, you have not spoken as you ought about me" (42:7).

The purpose of the book of Job (that is, the poetic dialogue) is to confront human suffering in a world created by God. Job insists throughout that there must be some satisfactory answer to this question. But he never finds it. The book of Job never offers us an intellectual, philosophical answer to the question of human suffering. Instead, it does something else. Job has dared to say things that are scandalous and border on blasphemy. He has accused God of being his enemy and being unjust. Such charges cannot go unanswered. Thus, God appears finally to correct Job's error and be vindicated, though at the same time God acknowledges Job's righteousness. Job's questioning, petulance, and anger melt away in the heat of God's overwhelming rhetorical questions. Job, who has only known of God by "the hearing of the ears," now confronts

God face to face in personal encounter. God is now no longer simply the object of formal piety but is also a living, inescapable presence. The poet's purpose, therefore, is to call in question the friends' traditional explanation of suffering and show that it is inadequate. Yet, the poet does not propose a new solution and so is not engaging in theodicy. The existence of both God and suffering remains a mystery.

But this intellectual mystery is transformed by an even greater mystery—that of the divine-human encounter. God's appearing to Job affirms Job's self-worth. Job maintains his integrity in the face of powerful pressures to conform and compromise. Job therefore exemplifies the "courage to be." God's address to Job affirms Job's self-valuation and invests Job with new dignity and honor. Job is no longer the wealthy, pious, wise man. He is now the one-addressed-by-God, the one who because of his integrity and refusal to conform is worthy now to stand in the presence of God.

Chapter 2

Why Does God Allow This?
The Attack on Job's Integrity Begins

The Book of Job struggles with one of the most profound questions we can ask—why do people suffer? There are only two possible answers. First, there is no adequate answer—suffering just occurs by chance, and the sufferer is simply unlucky. Second, there is an adequate answer—suffering serves some meaningful purpose, and the sufferer can learn to bear the suffering without being broken. With regard to the first option, there is not much more to be said. We just suffer, that's all. We must bear it the best we can. Suffering is pointless, purposeless, without any redeeming meaning. With regard to the second answer, however, further questions do arise. Do we, for example, know what the answer is, or is it hidden from us? What method is appropriate for discovering the answer? Is there more than one answer? How can we decide which of several answers is the best? And even if we do somehow come to know the answer, what difference does it really make?

The poet who wrote the Book of Job believed there was an adequate answer to the question of suffering. This is the fundamental assumption underlying the poetic dialogue. But the poet was not writing a philosophical text and therefore did not begin (as a philosopher would) by raising questions to be answered. Instead, the poet begins with an anguished and angry cry of pain.

Job's Curse: The Threat of Meaninglessness

After seven nights of sitting surrounded by his friends, Job "broke his silence and cursed the day of his birth":

> Let the day perish in which I was born,
> > and the night that said,
> > "A man child is conceived."
> Let that day be darkness!
> > May God above not seek it,
> > or light shine on it.
> Let gloom and deep darkness claim it.
> > Let clouds settle upon it;
> > let the blackness of the day terrify it.
> That night—let thick darkness seize it!
> > let it not rejoice among the days of the year;
> > let it not come into the number of the months.
> Yes, let that night be barren;
> > let no joyful cry be heard in it.
> Let those curse it who curse the Sea,
> > those who are skilled to rouse up Leviathan.
> Let the stars of its dawn be dark;
> > let it hope for light, but have none;
> > may it not see the eyelids of the morning—
> because it did not shut the doors of my mother's womb,
> > and hide trouble from my eyes. (3:3-10)

These are astonishing, stunning words. Nothing in the prologue has prepared us for this sudden outpouring of bitter grief. The images are breathtaking. Job cries for the day of his birth to be obliterated from the calendar, swallowed up in darkness, as if it had never been. When that day comes around again in the regular sequence of days, he wants it to be darkness not light, and he invokes every way the light of day may be obscured—fog, dark clouds, an eclipse of the sun. (In the REB translation, verse 5a reads: "May gloom and deep darkness claim it again, may cloud smother that day, blackness eclipse its sun.") Job invokes God—who established the orderly progression of day and night and who calls each day forth in its proper sequence—to skip this day altogether when its time comes around again. What has happened to

Job, in other words, is so terrifying in its implications that it threatens even the order God established in creation.

Job not only curses the day of his birth, he also curses the night of his conception. It too should perish, be obliterated. Human history should be as if that night had never occurred. Specifically, Job calls down two curses on this night. The first is that its darkness be utter darkness—"thick darkness" with no stars at all, darkness unrelieved by the promise of dawn, a never-ending darkness. Job's first curse on this night, in other words, is that it will never wake up. The second curse is that this night be barren forever, a night when no cry of joy is heard—that is, a night in which no child is conceived, much less conceived in joy. Job emphasizes his double curse on this night by invoking magicians and wizards, capable of pronouncing the most potent of spells, to curse it along with him. This invocation of spellbinders illustrates the depth of Job's bitterness and anguish, for the Hebrews abominated such workers of magic, who were to be put to death for practicing their black arts. In other words, Job is so desperate for his plight not to occur again that he goes so far as to invoke outlawed powers.

The poet's skill is seen not only in the stunning images used but also in the control exhibited over material that threatens to get out of hand. The controlling device is the parallelism of verse 3 which imposes order over the whole passage. Verse 3a curses the day of Job's birth, verse 3b curses the night of Job's conception. Verses 4-5 expand on the curse of the day, and verses 6-10 expand on the curse of the night. And within each verse itself, there is a parallelism too complex to analyze here. Suffice it to say that this highly complex interplay of parallelism imposes unity on Job's wildly emotional outpouring and contributes to its powerful effect—one not unlike that of the opening movement of Beethoven's Ninth Symphony, an effect of controlled passion.

This passage is just the opening movement of Job's symphony of suffering. If his existence could not have been cut off at its very beginning, then perhaps it might have been cut off at birth:

> Why did I not die at birth,
>   come forth from the womb and expire?

> Why were there knees to receive me,
>   or breasts for me to suck?
> Now I would be lying down and quiet;
>   I would be asleep; then I would be at rest
> with kings and counselors of the earth
>   who rebuild ruins for themselves,
> or with princes who have gold,
>   who fill their houses with silver.
> Or why was I not buried like a stillborn child,
>   like an infant that never sees the light?
> There the wicked cease from troubling,
>   and the weary are at rest.
> There the prisoners are at ease together;
>   they do not hear the voice of the taskmaster.
> The small and the great are there,
>   and the slaves are free from their masters. (3:11-19)

Once again Job's words roll like thunder. Job is saying he would have been better off going straight to Sheol, the abode of the dead. Existence there was a shadowy existence, cut off from the full vitality of earthly existence and cut off from God. It was not a place of punishment, neither was it a place of reward. The Hebrews put a premium on long life partly because existence in Sheol paled into insignificance in comparison with the delights of existence on earth. Sheol is the great leveller where there are no distinctions between kings and princes and the lowliest laborer. Job's earlier well-being has been shattered by his present anguish. Sheol is at least quiet, a place of rest. Thus, however inferior existence may be there, it is preferable to Job's present condition.

Job ends his soliloquy with a bitter questioning of why people suffering as he does are compelled to go on living:

> Why is light given to one in misery,
>   and life to the bitter in soul,
> who long for death, but it does not come,
>   and dig for it more than for hidden treasures;
> who rejoice exceedingly,
>   and are glad when they find the grave?
> Why is light given to one who cannot see the way,
>   whom God has fenced in?

For my sighing comes like my bread,
  and my groanings are poured out like water.
Truly the thing that I fear comes upon me,
  and what I dread befalls me.
I am not at ease, nor am I quiet;
  I have no rest; but trouble comes. (3:20-26)

People suffering like Job "long for death." This verb is used elsewhere of robbers who lie in wait for their victim. So one who suffers like Job hopes to ambush death. Death is the victim attacked by the sufferer. It is also a hidden treasure the sufferer seeks impatiently and obsessively. It is the cause of rejoicing and gladness and exultation. Life for one like Job is like wandering blindly in unfamiliar territory. Life is "hedged in" for one like Job. (In the prologue, Satan had accused God of "hedging Job around"—that is, putting up a protective fence. But God's hedging has been to hedge Job *in*, to put him in a situation of suffering with no way out.) Every evil thing Job had ever thought possible has come true. And in ironic contrast to the existence in Sheol which he has just described, he cannot rest at all, he cannot escape his suffering even for a moment.

The last section of Job's curse introduces a subtle but significant shift in Job's perspective. Thus far he has spoken in the first person singular, but in verse 20 and following he speaks in the third person. Job is beginning to see that his personal problem may also be a problem for others, that there may be a more general application for his questions. Job's perspective is beginning to broaden from the narrow perspective of "Why did this happen to *me?*" to the wider perspective of "Why does this ever happen to *anyone?*" He is beginning to recognize his kinship with the many people who suffer as he does but are unable to articulate their feelings.

In the context of the poetry, we do not know exactly what Job's situation is. The poet does not describe the calamities that befell Job (though 7:5 indicates he suffers from a skin disease). Because of the prologue, we assume that Job has lost his wealth, his family, and his social status. But the particulars of his suffering are really unimportant, because the real source of his anguish is deeper than any particular loss or pain. It is not the suffering itself, but rather what this suffering implies that calls forth his cry of anguish. Job had based his life on the implicit belief that the universe is orderly and reasonable; that he could know that order and conduct his life in accord with it, and that, as a consequence, he could confidently expect certain good things from life. Job had believed in an ultimate purpose of life accessible to him. But now his undeserved and unexplained suffering calls all that into question and threatens to plunge him into cynical despair.

Another poet, Thomas Hardy, in another poem, "Hap," articulates the kind of despair which threatens Job:

> If but some vengeful god would call to me
> From up the sky, and laugh: "Thou suffering thing,
> Know that thy sorrow is my ecstasy,
> That thy love's loss is my hate's profiting!"
>
> Then would I bear it, clench myself, and die
> Steeled by the sense of ire unmerited;
> Half-eased in that a Powerfuller than I
> Had willed and meted me the tears I shed.
>
> But not so. How arrives it joy lies slain,
> And why unblooms the best hope ever sown?
> —Crass Casualty obstructs the sun and rain,
> And dicing Time for gladness casts a moan. . . .
> These purblind Doomsters had as readily strown
> Blisses about my pilgrimage as pain.[1]

For Hardy, in this poem, the fact of suffering implies a chaotic universe of chance where "crass casualty" and "dicing time" determine whether or not we will be happy. Happiness is totally a matter of good luck. Suffering is totally a matter of bad luck. The fact that suffering just happens, in Hardy's view, makes it intolerable. It would be better if there were some malevolent deity whose purpose is to cause our suffering. Then, at least, we could be fortified and our burden of suffering be "half-eased." Then, at least, there would be an explanation. Instead, we must live with the realization that we are just unlucky when suffering comes. In other

---

[1] Walter Houghton and Robert Strange, eds., *Victorian Poetry and Poetics* (Boston: Houghton Mifflin Company, 1959) 784.

words, Hardy believed that there is no explanation for suffering, and the life of the sufferer is meaningless.

Job, too, is threatened with the possibility that nihilism is the truth about human existence. At the end of his curse, we do not yet know which of the two possible options he will take. Neither do his friends. But he has said enough to send ripples of fear and concern through the placid surface of his friends' orderly existence. This cry of anguish must be answered.

Eliphaz and Job

Job's friends were not expecting, and thus were not prepared for, Job's curse. They had come to play a well-defined social role (the comforter) and they were expecting Job to play his role (the mourner). The mourner's role was to lament his or her fate in a set poetic form which included the following: (1) invocation of God's help in time of trouble; (2) description of the cause of mourning and lamentation; (3) either confession of wrongdoing or assertion of innocence; and (4) expression of confidence in God. But Job's curse did not follow this pattern. It was simply a cry of anguish that his suffering is so great that all meaning in his life has been obliterated. How can the friends respond to this? Job has not played his role according to the rules, so what now is their role?

We must imagine, I think, a long uncomfortable silence after Job finishes speaking. We must imagine the friends shifting uneasily as they consider how to respond. Finally Eliphaz—probably the oldest and thus considered the wisest—begins gingerly to feel his way to a response:

> If one ventures a word with you, will you be offended?
> But who can keep from speaking?
> See, you have instructed many, you have strengthened
>   the weak hands.
> Your words have supported those who were stumbling,
> and you have made firm the feeble knees.
> But now it has come to you, and you are impatient;
> it touches you, and you are dismayed.
> Is not your fear of God your confidence,

> and the integrity of your ways your hope?
> Think now, who that was innocent ever perished?
> Or where were the upright cut off?
> As I have seen, those who plow iniquity
> and sow trouble reap the same.
> By the breath of God they perish, and by the blast
>   of his anger they are consumed. (4:2-9)

Eliphaz first recalls how Job himself had comforted others in time of trouble and chides Job for not following the good advice he has given. In other words, Job is being inconsistent. When adversity touches him he loses patience. Job, who has counseled others to maintain their faith in time of trouble, seems to be on the brink of losing his when trouble visits him. Eliphaz clearly has not caught the depth of Job's suffering. He clearly does not perceive what Job has seen—that suffering such as his calls everything he has believed into question. There is a great gulf—never bridged—fixed between Job's perception and that of his friends.

Eliphaz then articulates the basic assumption the three friends share throughout the dialogue: this kind of calamity does not befall an innocent person; one reaps what one sows; the innocent do not perish, only the guilty. Eliphaz states this assumption explicitly, and the implication is inescapable—Job must have done something to deserve what has happened. In other words, there is an explanation of why people suffer: they suffer because they have sinned.

Eliphaz senses, perhaps, the inadequacy of this position and hastens on to another idea.

> Now a word came stealing to me, my ear received the whisper of it.
> Amid thoughts from visions of the night,
>   when deep sleep falls on mortals,
> dread came upon me, and trembling,
>   which made all my bones shake.
> A spirit glided past my face; the hair of my flesh bristled.
> It stood still, but I could not discern its appearance.
> A form was before my eyes; there was silence, then I heard a voice:
> "Can mortals be righteous before God?
> Can human beings be pure before their Maker?

> Even in his servants he puts no trust,
>   and his angels he charges with error;
> how much more those who live in houses of clay,
> whose foundation is in the dust, who are crushed like a moth.
> Between morning and evening they are destroyed;
> they perish forever without any regarding it.
> Their tent-cord is plucked up within them,
> and they die devoid of wisdom." (4:12-21)

This is one of the strangest passages in the Book of Job. With terse economy of words the poet makes us feel Eliphaz's uncanny, supernatural experience. It is doubly strange that Eliphaz, the proponent of wisdom, appeals to a mystical vision instead of experience. This double strangeness does not, however, obscure the main idea. Human beings are impure and unrighteous before God their Maker. Our mortality is such that we cannot be trusted. We can be snuffed out, destroyed as easily as a house whose foundation is dust or a moth which can disappear overnight. God does not even trust the heavenly servants or messengers (angels). And compared to them, we are practically worthless.

Eliphaz then comments on his vision:

> Call now; is there anyone who will answer you?
> To which of the holy ones will you turn?
> Surely vexation kills the fool, and jealousy slays the simple.
> I have seen fools taking root, but suddenly I cursed their dwelling.
> Their children are far from safety, they are crushed in the gate,
>   and there is no one to deliver them.
> The hungry eat their harvest, and they take it even out of the
>   thorns; and the thirsty pant after their wealth.
> For misery does not come from the earth,
>   nor does trouble sprout from the ground;
> but human beings are born to trouble just as sparks fly upward.
> (5:1-7)

Let Job call to one of the heavenly hosts for help, and he will discover the truth Eliphaz saw in his vision. Even mighty, heavenly beings can't help him. Compared to them, human mortality is such that human existence is fragile. One's prosperity can suddenly be turned to disaster. The fool doesn't recognize this and so

is unprepared when disaster strikes. The truth is that trouble is as
inevitable for human beings as it is inevitable that sparks fly upward. (Verse 7 may also be translated "as the birds fly upward"—
in either case the meaning is the same.) Because human beings are
creatures made of earth they will inevitably have troubles. Why,
then, is Job complaining? Trouble and suffering are to be expected. It is folly, therefore, to question or carp.

Eliphaz is offering here a second explanation of suffering—
not only do people suffer because they have sinned, they also suffer because it is inevitable for creatures made of such lowly stuff
as matter (clay and dust) to suffer. In neither case is Job's questioning justified. (Notice that Eliphaz's comment on his vision re-
verts to the usual Wisdom appeal—human experience.)

Eliphaz ends his first speech with some sage advice:

> As for me, I would seek God,
>   and to God I would commit my cause.
> He does great things and unsearchable,
>   marvelous things without number.
> He gives rain on the earth and sends waters on the fields;
> he sets on high those who are lowly,
>   and those who mourn are lifted to safety.
> He frustrates the devices of the crafty,
>   so that their hands achieve no success.
> He takes the wise in their own craftiness;
>   and the schemes of the wily are brought to a quick end. (5:8-13)

Job should throw himself on the mercy of God, who does things
beyond our ability to understand. And Job should also avoid trying to be too crafty or cunning. That is, Job should be careful asking all these questions, expressing such deep and bitter anguish.
The proper attitude is that of supplication, not questioning.
Furthermore, Job should change his attitude toward his suffering:

> How happy is the one whom God reproves;
>   therefore do not despise the discipline of the Almighty.
> For he wounds, but he binds up;
>   he strikes, but his hands heal. (5:17-18)

Job's suffering is really discipline from God (though for what purpose, Eliphaz does not say). Thus, Job should actually be grateful for his suffering!

Finally, Eliphaz ends his first speech with the sage's imprimatur: "See, we have searched this out; it is true. Hear, and know it for yourself" (5:27). So Job should not question but just take Eliphaz's word for it.

Job's First Answer to Eliphaz

Eliphaz's first speech is as cool and rational and logical as Job's curse had been hot and emotional. He begins with the personal appeal to Job to remember his own advice to others on similar occasions. Then he states the main point of view he and the other two friends will defend—that sin inevitably results in suffering. This is bolstered by a secondary appeal to the lowly, despicable status of human nature, which means that trouble and suffering are inevitable and which is proved both by mystical vision and ordinary experience. Then Eliphaz draws the conclusion that Job's only recourse is to throw himself on God's mercy, (gratefully) accept his suffering as discipline from God, and hope that God will (eventually) restore him to his previous status. His attitude seems to be that Job will surely see the wisdom of this advice once he begins to think about it. Job's suffering has temporarily deranged him, Eliphaz seems to believe, and all he needs is for someone to give him good advice. Then Job will see the light and back away from the dangerous intellectual and religious precipice towards which he has so closely careened.

Unfortunately, Eliphaz has simply failed to perceive Job's problem. The confident assertion with which he ended his speech is blasted by Job's response:

> O that my vexation were weighed, and all my calamity laid in the
>   balances!
> For then it would be heavier than the sand of the sea;
>   therefore my words have been rash.
> For the arrows of the Almighty are in me;
>   my spirit drinks their poison;
>   the terrors of God are arrayed against me.

> Does the wild ass bray over its grass,
>   or the ox low over its fodder?
> Can that which is tasteless be eaten without salt,
>   or is there any flavor in the juice of mallows?
> My appetite refuses to touch them;
>   they are like food that is loathsome to me. (6:2-7)

At first Job seems to be ignoring Eliphaz. It is almost as if he is speaking to himself. He uses, once again, powerful images. His burden weighs more than the sands of the sea. (The REB translation of verses 2 and 3 is much more forceful than the NRSV: "If only the grounds for my resentment might be weighed, and my misfortunes placed with them on the scales! For they would outweigh the sands of the sea: what wonder if my words are frenzied!") He is God's archery target. The arrows of the Almighty are doubly hurtful because they are tipped with poison. God is arrayed against Job like a besieging army whose purpose is to wear him away or wear him down. God, in other words, is behaving like an enemy toward Job. The effect of God's attack is to sicken Job and so, beginning in verse 5, he changes the imagery. He likens himself to a braying ass or a lowing ox. These images indicate a serious deprivation. The wild ass does not bray nor the ox low when it has adequate nourishment. Since Job is braying and lowing, something must be seriously wrong. His sickened condition is such that no food appeals to him. It is all repulsive. Food that should nourish him he is unable to swallow.

Though these opening words do not seem directed toward Eliphaz, they really constitute an answer to his injunction to petition God. How can I look to God for help, Job is saying, when it is God who has done this to me? Then Job states explicitly the request implicit in his curse:

> O that I might have my request, and that God would grant my
>   desire;
> that it would please God to crush me,
>   that he would let loose his hand and cut me off!
> This would be my consolation;
>   I would even exult in unrelenting pain;
>   for I have not denied the words of the Holy One.

What is my strength, that I should wait?
>And what is my end, that I should be patient?
Is my strength the strength of stones,
>or is my flesh bronze?
In truth I have no help in me,
>and any resource is driven from me. (6:8-13)

Why doesn't God just go ahead and kill me? Job asks. His curse had implied his desire for death, and now he explicitly asks for it. He no longer has the strength to bear his suffering. The image of verse 12 is of stone being cut by a carver or bronze being shaped by a sculptor. If you say God's discipline is to shape me and form me, he says to Eliphaz, then you have forgotten an important detail. My material is flesh and blood, not stone or bronze. God's supposed cutting and shaping is something I *feel*, unlike these materials which feel nothing. So Job answers Eliphaz's assertion that he should be happy for God's discipline. He can't be grateful for *this* suffering.

Then Job addresses Eliphaz directly:

Those who withhold kindness from a friend
>forsake the fear of the Almighty.
My companions are treacherous like a torrent-bed,
>like freshets that pass away,
that run dark with ice,
>turbid with melting snow.
In time of heat they disappear;
>when it is hot, they vanish from their place.
The caravans turn aside from their course;
>they go up into the waste, and perish. . . .
Such you now have become to me;
>you see my calamity, and are afraid.
Have I said, "Make me a gift"?
>Or, "From your wealth offer a bribe for me"?
Or, "Save me from an opponent's hand"?
>Or, "Ransom me from the hand of oppressors"?
(6:14-18, 21-23)

Job's accusation turns on a single sustained image—the dry stream bed. Merchant caravans depended on streams flowing at certain times of the year. On occasion something would block the stream and keep it from flowing, so the stream was dry when it should have had water. The merchants who depended on the stream would thus face death because of the lack of water. Such streams are treacherous, not to be depended on. And so, Job says, are you my friends. I thought you would understand, but you don't.

Eliphaz has spoken out of fear. His accusation of Job is a defensive mechanism to cope with the threat Job presents to him. If such calamities can befall such a person, then they may happen to anyone. But if Eliphaz can accuse Job of some wrongdoing, then he can be reassured that Job deserves his suffering. This is Job's response:

> Teach me, and I will be silent;
>> make me understand how I have gone wrong.
> How forceful are honest words!
>> But your reproof, what does it reprove?
> Do you think that you can reprove words,
>> as if the speech of the desperate were wind?
> You would even cast lots over the orphan,
>> and bargain over your friend.
> But now, be pleased to look at me,
>> for I will not lie to your face.
> Turn, I pray, let no wrong be done.
>> Turn now, my vindication is at stake. (6:24-29)

Eliphaz has implied that Job was sinful. Well, Job retorts, don't just insinuate—tell me plainly where I have sinned. He is confident that his friend cannot do this. Eliphaz's unjust accusation is comparable to assailing the most defenseless member of society, the orphan. Job is like an orphan now without any external resources. He expected compassion from his friends. Instead, he has been attacked. His friends have added yet one more burden for Job to bear, their lack of understanding. So Job makes a desperate appeal. Just *look* at me, he says, am I likely to be telling you lies in *this* state? Job is at the nadir of his suffering. His integrity is in question by the people who know him best. He knows he is innocent. Yet all of the evidence, according to the accepted beliefs of his day, is against him.

Job speaks to himself at the beginning of his response and to Eliphaz in the middle. There is yet another character in this drama, the most important one—at the end Job addresses God:

> Therefore I will not restrain my mouth;
>> I will speak in the anguish of my spirit;
>> I will complain in the bitterness of my soul.
> Am I the Sea, or the Dragon,
>> that you set a guard over me?
> When I say, "My bed will comfort me,
>> my couch will ease my complaint,"
> then you scare me with dreams
>> and terrify me with visions,
> so that I would choose strangling
>> and death rather than this body.
> I loathe my life; I would not live forever.
>> Let me alone, for my days are a breath.
> What are human beings, that you make so much of them,
>> that you set your mind on them,
> visit them every morning,
>> test them every moment?
> Will you not look away from me for a while,
>> let me alone until I swallow my spittle?
> If I sin, what do I do to you, you watcher of humanity?
>> Why have you made me your target?
>> Why have I become a burden to you?
> Why do you not pardon my transgression
>> and take away my iniquity?
> For now I shall lie in the earth;
>> you will seek me, but I shall not be. (7:11-21)

This address to God begins with Job's self-justification. He is saying such wild things because of his great distress and bitterness. Then he asks, Who am I to have become so significant an object of God's attentions? Am I the monster of the deep to deserve God's careful watch over me? Job alludes here to the common Near Eastern myth that the ocean represents the forces of chaos and destruction which would reverse God's creative order. Thus, the monster of the deep requires God's constant watchfulness, lest there be an outbreak of disorder. Is Job that much of a danger to

God? To show the absurdity of such a question, Job describes his daily existence. At night his sleep is troubled with frightening dreams. During the day he is all too conscious of his sufferings which choke him. At this point Job parodies Psalm 8:4:

> What are human beings that you are mindful of them,
> mortals that you care for them?

Psalm 8 expresses grateful wonder that God should place humanity at such a level of preeminence in creation. Job's parody is ironic in that he is appealing for a little less preeminence before God. God watches Job so closely that he cannot even swallow his spit without God knowing. Job ends with a question to God: Even if I had sinned, how much would that have injured you? Then Job requests that God pardon his offense, whatever it may be; not because he has committed a sin, but because he will soon die and it will be too late to pardon him. God will realize too late the mistake of persecuting Job. Job will be dead and beyond the reach of God's pardon.

This cycle of speeches by Job is a masterpiece of controlled passion. It is organized in the following way: 6:1-13 is a general description of Job's calamity and suffering, parallel to 7:1-10, a general description of the human condition (with Job being a particular instance of the general). 6:14-30 is a direct address to Eliphaz, paralleled in 7:11-21 by a direct address to God. The poet exerts further control by having Job's outbursts answer Eliphaz's main points. Job cannot rely on God, because God is the source of his suffering, God is his enemy. Job cannot be grateful for his suffering as a discipline from God, because it is so out of proportion to any useful rehabilitative measures. And Job explicitly denies the implication that he has sinned and thus deserves what has happened. Finally, the *movement* of Job's response exerts control. That is, Job moves from addressing the three friends to addressing God, and this movement occurs (as we shall see) in all of Job's responses in this first cycle of speeches. This, indeed, is the movement of the entire poem, from Job's situation with the questions it raises to God's appearance at the end.

Chapter 3

The Attack Continues

Bildad, the second friend, is incensed at Job's reply to Eliphaz. Eliphaz had shown some sensitivity toward Job, at least at the beginning of his speech. Bildad, however, shows none and attacks Job with sarcasm.

Bildad and Job

Job's words, Bildad says, are the "long-winded ramblings of an old man." Job's sons, he asserts, deserved everything they got. Bildad rightly sees that Job questions God's justice. And Bildad will have none of that—it is unthinkable that God could be unjust. Bildad then offers the traditional advice to Job: seek God and throw yourself on God's mercy.

> For inquire now of bygone generations,
>   and consider what their ancestors have found;
> for we are but of yesterday, and we know nothing,
>   for our days on earth are but a shadow.
> Will they not teach you and tell you
>   and utter words out of their understanding?
> Can papyrus grow where there is no marsh?
>   Can reeds flourish where there is no water?
> While yet in flower and not cut down,
>   they wither before any other plant.
> Such are the paths of all who forget God;
>   the hope of the godless shall perish.

> Their confidence is gossamer,
>> a spider's house their trust.
> If one leans against its house, it will not stand;
>> if one lays hold of it, it will not endure.
> The wicked thrive before the sun,
>> and their shoots spread over the garden.
> Their roots twine around the stoneheap;
>> they live among the rocks.
> If they are destroyed from their place,
>> then it will deny them, saying,
>> "I have never seen you."
> See, these are their happy ways,
>> and out of the earth still others will spring. (8:8-19)

Eliphaz had expressed confidence in his own opinion ("We have enquired into all this, and so it is. . . ."), but Bildad will have none of this. In contrast, his confidence is in the traditional wisdom of the past, the accumulated experience of the ancestors. Bildad is the archetypal conservative looking askance at the new and modern. (It would be interesting to know what he really thinks of Eliphaz's mystical vision.) At any rate, Bildad is confident that he is right because older generations have taught that people are punished for their sins. This is as certain as it is that reeds cannot grow without water or that they wither more quickly than any other plant. The godless person's confidence is as substantial as a spider's web. The godless person's prosperity is like the lush growth of a plant on stony ground—it is easily uprooted because it has no depth.

This summary of ancient wisdom was prefaced by Bildad's sarcastic advice. He closes with a repetition of that advice, couched this time in less offensive language, as if he has become aware that he came on too strongly at the beginning. God will not turn away a blameless person, Bildad assures Job. But even this assurance has its sting. All the wisdom of the past points to Job's *not* being blameless.

Once again Job chooses not to answer his accuser directly at first. He begins with a profound meditation on the inscrutability of the ways of God, who causes the mountains to move, who commands the sun and stars. What mortal could possibly contend

with such an awesome reality as the reality of God? Yet, that is precisely what Job is doing:

> Look, he passes by me, and I do not see him;
>> he moves on, but I do not perceive him.
> He snatches away; who can stop him?
>> Who will say to him, "What are you doing?"
> God will not turn back his anger;
>> the helpers of Rahab bowed beneath him.
> How then can I answer him,
>> choosing my words with him?
> Though I am innocent, I cannot answer him,
>> I must appeal for mercy to my accuser.
> If I summoned him and he answered me,
>> I do not believe that he would listen to my voice.
> For he crushes me with a tempest,
>> and multiplies my wounds without cause;
> he will not let me get my breath,
>> but fills me with bitterness.
> If it is a contest of strength, he is the strong one!
>> If it is a matter of justice, who can summon him?
> Though I am innocent, my own mouth would condemn me;
>> though I am blameless, he would prove me perverse.
> I am blameless; I do not know myself;
>> I loathe my life.
> It is all one; therefore I say,
>> he destroys both the blameless and the wicked.
> When disaster brings sudden death,
>> he mocks at the calamity of the innocent.
> The earth is given into the hand of the wicked;
>> he covers the eyes of its judges—
>> if it is not he, who then is it? (9:11-24)

Once again Job astonishes us with his daring. He is challenging
God, and he is fully aware of the impossibility of his task. No one
can command God to appear, no one can command God to be
still so that God's accuser can speak accusations. Even though Job
is right, God would not listen to him because God is too busy
raining blows on him for trifles. And how could one compel God
to appear? By force? No, God is stronger. (Job's reference to Rahab

is to a mythological dragon who was vanquished when the heavens and earth were created. Rahab represents one of the most powerful forces Job can conceive.) By appealing to justice?—Ah, there Job has indeed raised the basic issue at stake. God is supposed to be just. If Job *is* innocent, then a just God *would* appear and hear his case. But God has not answered Job. And since Job is innocent, he is compelled to the conclusion that God is not just. Though this is blasphemy, he cannot help but entertain this possibility. In other words, Job considers the possibility that God is malevolent—the possibility Thomas Hardy raised and rejected in "Hap."

But this horrible thought leads Job to consider a new possibility—the idea of an arbitrator:

> For he is not a mortal, as I am, that I might answer him,
>   that we should come to trial together.
> Would that there were an umpire between us, [1]
>   who might lay his hand on us both.
> If he would take his rod away from me,
>   and not let dread of him terrify me,
> then I would speak without fear of him,
>   for I know I am not what I am thought to be. (9:32-35)

This idea is, of course, inconsistent with his earlier assertions. No one has the power to compel God; Job has already admitted this. Yet he cannot escape from his sense of the rightness of his cause, which convinces him that an impartial arbitrator would find in his favor. (This appeal to an arbitrator is an important step in the evolution of Job's thought.)

Job ends his response to Bildad the same way he ended his response to Eliphaz—with a direct address to God:

> I loathe my life; I will give free utterance to my complaint;
>   I will speak in the bitterness of my soul.

[1]This is the NRSV alternate reading of verse 33, which is supported by the REB, the NAB, and the NIV. The translation preferred by the NRSV is "There is no umpire between us" (and is supported by the NJB). I prefer the alternate reading here because Job alludes to a third party intermediary in 16:18-22.

I will say to God, Do not condemn me;
    let me know why you contend against me.
Does it seem good to you to oppress,
    to despise the work of your hands
    and favor the schemes of the wicked?
Do you have eyes of flesh?
    Do you see as humans see?
Are your days like the days of mortals,
    or your years like human years,
that you seek out my iniquity
    and search for my sin,
although you know that I am not guilty,
    and there is no one to deliver out of your hand? (10:1-7)

Job is desperate to know the reasons why God has turned on him. He is so sickened by what has happened that he believes nothing worse could befall him regardless of what he says, so he will give free reign to his grief. Does God attack him in order to gain some advantage? What could that possibly be? Job has served God faithfully, now God is destroying all the fruit of that devotion. Job implicitly excuses his friends for their failure to stand by him. After all, they have eyes of flesh, they see only as mere mortals see. Isn't God's seeing different? Doesn't God see into the human heart and know people as they really are? Surely, God knows that Job is innocent.

Job turns from logical argument to emotional appeal:

Your hands fashioned and made me;
    and now you turn and destroy me.
Remember that you fashioned me like clay;
    and will you turn me to dust again?
Did you not pour me out like milk
    and curdle me like cheese?
You clothed me with skin and flesh,
    and knit me together with bones and sinews.
You have granted me life and steadfast love,
    and your care has preserved my spirit. (10:8-12)

Job calls God to remember the tender care with which he was made. He calls God to remember the continuing favor he had

received at God's hands and the providential watchcare God had
provided in the past. How can God then turn on Job and destroy
him? Then a horrible thought comes to Job, an answer to his
question:

> Yet these things you hid in your heart;
>   I know that this was your purpose.
> If I sin, you watch me,
>   and do not acquit me of my iniquity.
> If I am wicked, woe to me!
>   If I am righteous I cannot lift up my head,
> for I am filled with disgrace
>   and look upon my affliction.
> Bold as a lion you hunt me;
>   you repeat your exploits against me.
> You renew your witnesses against me,
>   and increase your vexation toward me,
>   you bring fresh troops against me. (10:13-17)

The horrible thought is that God has set Job up by granting him
the earlier lavish blessings in order to make their loss all the more
intense and intolerable. God's earlier kindness was calculated to
intensify the suffering Job experienced when God turned on him.
(The REB makes this clearer than the NRSV in verses 13-14: "Yet
this was the secret purpose of your heart, and I know it was your
intent: that if I sinned, you would be watching me and would not
absolve me of my guilt.") Job here seems to believe that God's intent toward him was malevolent from the very beginning. It did
not matter whether he was wicked or righteous, God's intention
was always to set upon him like an enemy and relentlessly pursue
him, bringing "fresh forces to the attack." None of this makes
sense to Job. But if this is the way things have been, then Job
pleads for at least a brief respite before he dies.

Zophar and Job

Zophar, the third friend, now takes his turn. He begins by re-
buking Job for talking nonsense—that is, for claiming to be innocent in the sight of God. What Job needs is for God to instruct

him in wisdom, for it is obvious that Job is talking like a fool. Then Zophar expresses his particular point of view:

> Can you find out the deep things of God?
>> Can you find out the limit of the Almighty?
> It is higher than heaven—what can you do?
>> Deeper than Sheol—what can you know?
> Its measure is longer than the earth,
>> and broader than the sea.
> If he passes through, and imprisons,
>> and assembles for judgment, who can hinder him?
> For he knows those who are worthless;
>> when he sees iniquity, will he not consider it? (11:7-11)

Eliphaz had confidence in his own experience and that of his peers. Bildad had confidence in the experience of the sages of old. But Zophar has no confidence whatsoever in the human ability to know the ways of God. Thus, Job's insistence that God appear for questioning is an outrage to Zophar's theological sensibilities. For Zophar, no one has the right to question God. God's ways are mysterious and past finding out. Whatever God wants to do, God may and will do, and no one should try to comprehend it. Zophar takes refuge in irrationalism—whatever happens, no matter how awful, is God's will—and thereby contradicts Job's desire for an explanation.

Job's response begins with sarcasm: "No doubt you are intelligent people, and when you die, wisdom will perish!" (12:1). The trouble with their wisdom is that it does not begin to comprehend Job's problem. So, Job's opening response to Zophar is to deny that the friends' point of view is really wisdom. It is not wisdom, first, because they are using him as a scapegoat. It is easy to attack him; he is helpless and without any resource but the inner conviction that he is right. Instead of turning their attention to real evildoers who are safe and sound, they find imaginary evil in one who is in no position to defend himself. Second, whatever truth they have spoken is not unique to them. Others know it. Even the lowliest creatures of the earth—cattle, birds, creatures that crawl, fish—know what the three friends know. Furthermore, if God is so unfettered by any constraint, as Zophar says, then God may be turning their wisdom upside down and playing them for the fool. God can make "counsellors behave like madmen" and turn "judges crazy" and rob "the old of their judgment" (12:17, 20). So, why could God not be deranging the minds of the three friends?

Job knows, as much as Zophar, the mysterious, inscrutable power of God. But Job also knows what Zophar doesn't, or has at least forgotten: God is supposed to be a God of justice, and if a God of justice, then a God who should be willing to listen to Job's case. So, Job says:

> But I would speak to the Almighty,
>> and I desire to argue my case with God.
> As for you, you whitewash with lies;
>> all of you are worthless physicians.
> If you would only keep silent,
>> that would be your wisdom!
> Hear now my reasoning,
>> and listen to the pleadings of my lips.
> Will you speak falsely for God,
>> and speak deceitfully for him?
> Will you show partiality toward him,
>> will you plead the case for God?
> Will it be well with you when he searches you out?
>> Or can you deceive him, as one person deceives another?
> He will surely rebuke you
>> if in secret you show partiality.
> Will not his majesty terrify you,
>> and the dread of him fall upon you?
> Your maxims are proverbs of ashes,
>> your defenses are defenses of clay.
> Let me have silence, and I will speak,
>> and let come on me what may.
> I will take my flesh in my teeth,
>> and put my life in my hand.
> See, he will kill me; I have no hope;
>> but I will defend my ways to his face.
> This will be my salvation,
>> that the godless shall not come before him.
> Listen carefully to my words,
>> and let my declaration be in your ears.

I have indeed prepared my case;
   I know that I shall be vindicated.
Who is there that will contend with me?
   For then I would be silent and die. (13:3-19)

Job's first point is that there is something terribly wrong with the friends' argument if they must deny the truth and assert falsehoods to defend the honor of God. That is, they are accusing Job of sin when they really know (if only they would admit it) that he is not guilty. Isn't it far more blasphemous for them to defend God with lies than it is for Job to accuse God of injustice when he can honestly see no other explanation? Surely, they dishonor God when they do so. Furthermore, they have so glibly talked of the majesty of God without really understanding the dreadful and terrible thing they have been talking about. Job contrasts himself with them. *He* knows that the things he has said are dangerous, that he has taken his life in his hands. But he is so convinced he is right that he is willing to run that risk.

Then Job addresses God:

Only grant two things to me,
   then I will not hide myself from your face:
withdraw your hand far from me,
   and do not let dread of you terrify me.
Then call, and I will answer;
   or let me speak, and you reply to me.
How many are my iniquities and my sins?
   Make me know my transgression and my sin.
Why do you hide your face,
   and count me as your enemy?
Will you frighten a windblown leaf
   and pursue dry chaff?
For me you write bitter things against me,
   and make me reap the iniquities of my youth.
You put my feet in the stocks,
   and watch all my paths;
      you set a bound to the soles of my feet.
One wastes away like a rotten thing,
   like a garment that is moth-eaten. (13:20-28)

Job's daring is astonishing. If God will (1) relieve his burden of suffering, and (2) give him the courage to stand in God's presence, then Job will willingly question God or be questioned by God. Ancient people believed that no one could stand in the presence of God and live—certainly no sinner. So Job is saying that he is willing to run the risk of forfeiting his life to learn the reasons for his suffering. Job then asks for the specific charges against him. So far God has refused to make such charges and God's face is hidden from Job—a sign of anger. God's anger against Job seems all out of proportion to what Job has done. It is as if God were chasing dry leaves blown by the wind—a pointless and futile task. Or, it is as if Job is a dry leaf blown by God's capricious fancy. Job is insignificant, in other words, and it is unworthy of God to persecute him in this way.

Job's response to Zophar culminates in a beautiful, profound soliloquy on the sovereignty of God and the finitude of human existence:

> A mortal, born of woman,
>> few of days and full of trouble,
> comes up like a flower and withers,
>> flees like a shadow and does not last.
> Do you fix your eyes on such a one?
>> Do you bring me into judgment with you?
> Who can bring a clean thing out of an unclean?
>> No one can.
> Since their days are determined,
>> and the number of the months is known to you,
>> and you have appointed the bounds that they cannot pass,
> look away from them, and desist,
>> that they may enjoy, like laborers, their days.
> For there is hope for a tree,
>> if it is cut down, that it will sprout again,
>> and that its shoots will not cease.
> Though its root grows old in the earth,
>> and its stump dies in the ground,
> yet at the scent of water it will bud
>> and put forth branches like a young plant.
> But mortals die, and are laid low;
>> humans expire, and where are they?

As waters fail from a lake,
    and a river wastes away and dries up,
so mortals lie down and do not rise again;
    until the heavens are no more, they will not awake
    or be roused out of their sleep.
Oh that you would hide me in Sheol,
    that you would conceal me until your wrath is past,
    that you would appoint me a set time, and remember me!
If mortals die, will they live again?
    All the days of my service I would wait
    until my release should come.
You would call, and I would answer you;
    you would long for the work of your hands.
For then you would not number my steps,
    you would not keep watch over my sin;
my transgression would be sealed up in a bag,
    and you would cover over my iniquity.
But the mountain falls and crumbles away,
    and the rock is removed from its place;
the waters wear away the stones;
    the torrents wash away the soil of the earth;
    so you destroy the hope of mortals.
You prevail forever against them, and they pass away;
    you change their countenance, and send them away.
Their children come to honor, and they do not know it;
    they are brought low, and it goes unnoticed.
They feel only the pain of their own bodies,
    and mourn only for themselves. (14:1-22)

Human existence is limited, fragile, full of dissatisfaction. It is as substantial as the bloom of a flower, or a shadow, or a moth-eaten garment. Human beings should not even draw any attention from God, so insignificant are they. Even a tree is superior to human beings in some ways—if it is cut down it may grow again, but when human existence is cut off that is the end. A human being can expect to rise from the dead when the heavens are no more—that is, never. If only God would hide Job in Sheol as a sanctuary for a while, the divine anger might turn away and God might eventually long to see "the work of your hands." That is, if God's anger could run its course, then God might remember the love once felt for Job. But instead God counts Job's every step and remembers Job's every offense. (The bag mentioned in verse 17 is probably a reference to a shepherd's bag in which the shepherd kept small stones used for counting sheep. God is, therefore, keeping track of Job's offenses like a shepherd counts sheep.) Job's sufferings have worn him away like a landslide wears down the side of a mountain or water wears away a stone. Everything Job might have hoped for has been wiped out.

Why Does God Allow This?

We have seen that there are two basic options as answers to the question of why people suffer. There is either no reason at all—suffering just happens by chance, and the sufferer is just unlucky—or there is a reason why suffering occurs, and suffering may, therefore, be made bearable. Job recognizes these options. His curse in chapter 3 expresses the overwhelming sense of meaninglessness with which his suffering threatens him. But nihilism does not, in the end, rout Job. Instead, he believes there is an answer to his question. Here is one point where Job and the friends agree.

The friends are more than ready to tell Job the reason for his sufferings. They know that suffering is a sign of sin. With irresistible logic they conclude that Job must have done something to deserve what has happened. Job wanted an answer, and here is an answer, one widely accepted and very plausible. It has the virtue of saving God's honor. It also has the virtue of showing Job what he ought to do—confess his sins and throw himself on God's mercy. Its disadvantage is that it is based on a false assumption. Job has *not* sinned and so has *not* deserved his suffering. There is nothing for him to confess.

Job believes, with his friends, that there is an answer but that their answer is wrong. So he explores other possibilities. One is that God may be malevolent, may actively wish Job ill. But this horrible thought is not satisfactory. Job does not really believe God wishes him ill. So, he tries out a new idea. If there were someone to arbitrate between him and God, then the truth would be known. An impartial third party would certainly see that Job was innocent and find in his favor. God would be compelled to admit

Job's innocence. But the idea of making God admit Job's innocence is, of course, absurd. No one can force God to do anything. So, at this point the idea of an arbitrator to vindicate Job does not seem to offer a solution. (It will, however, in the later cycles lead to Job's ultimate affirmation of God's justice.) By the end of the first cycle Job is still left without an answer to his question.

By the end of the first cycle Job is utterly alone. The incomprehensibility of his suffering isolates him from and sets him at odds with God. The dense insensitivity and callous cruelty of his friends who have come to comfort him has a similar effect. All Job can rely on at this moment is his unwavering sense of his own integrity. All he can rely on is his faith—tried to its limits—that he will be vindicated because he is right.

Chapter 4

The Second Cycle:
The Absence of God

As the dialogue grows more heated, it becomes increasingly obvious that neither Job nor his friends have an answer to Job's question and that ultimately the only satisfying answer will be one directly from God. Job, therefore, becomes more explicit in asking for an audience with God. But God remains silent and refuses to be known. Job experiences more deeply than before the profound absence of God in his suffering.

The speeches in the second cycle are shorter than those in the first. Job and his friends have established their respective positions in the first cycle, so in the second they repeat and elaborate their basic themes. The poet emphasizes God's absence by having Job address God only once.

Eliphaz and Job

Eliphaz begins the second cycle with a stinging rebuke

> Should the wise answer with windy knowledge,
>   and fill themselves with the east wind?
> Should they argue in unprofitable talk,
>   or in words with which they can do no good?
> But you are doing away with the fear of God,
>   and hindering meditation before God.

> For your iniquity teaches your mouth,
> > and you choose the tongue of the crafty.
> Your own mouth condemns you, and not I;
> > your own lips testify against you. (15:2-6)

No sensible person, Eliphaz asserts, would say the sort of things Job has said. Job's foolish speech has damned himself. He is being blasphemous and impious. He has banished orthodox religion ("the fear of God") and been guilty of overwhelming pride, arrogating to himself alone the right to speak to God. He is speaking lies.

Eliphaz intensifies the *ad hominem* attack:

> Are you the firstborn of the human race?
> > Were you brought forth before the hills?
> Have you listened in the council of God?
> > And do you limit wisdom to yourself?
> What do you know that we do not know?
> > What do you understand that is not clear to us?
> The gray-haired and the aged are on our side,
> > those older than your father.
> Are the consolations of God too small for you,
> > or the word that deals gently with you?
> Why does your heart carry you away,
> > and why do your eyes flash,
> so that you turn your spirit against God,
> > and let such words go out of your mouth?
> What are mortals, that they can be clean?
> > Or those born of woman, that they can be righteous?
> God puts no trust even in his holy ones,
> > and the heavens are not clean in his sight;
> how much less one who is abominable and corrupt,
> > one who drinks iniquity like water! (15:7-16)

Why would Job trust his own understanding? If he were the very first of the human race, perhaps he would then have some claim to wisdom. Does he listen in on God's secret council? No, of course not. Does he have the wisdom that comes with old age? No, the three friends are older than he and therefore wiser, and some of them are even older than Job's father. The truth is that Job is nothing but dust, and since God doesn't even trust the members of the heavenly council who are neither innocent nor pure, then why should God trust the likes of Job? And why should Job trust himself? Eliphaz waxes eloquent and overstates his case when he asserts dogmatically that human beings are "loathsome and corrupt." It is doubtful that Eliphaz thinks that about himself! Above all else, he simply cannot understand why Job has refused to take his advice and believe everything he has said. For in the middle of this tirade, he slips in a reference to his mystical vision (so chillingly related in 4:12-21). Surely, a vision should be authoritative. Eliphaz is saying, I've told you already how vile the human race in general is. Why do you keep asking these questions?

Eliphaz does not really believe God is so morally blind as to be unable to distinguish good human beings from bad ones, because in the remainder of his second speech he describes in vivid detail the terrible fate of the evildoer. The wicked have no peace of mind, they suffer black moods and get depressed. They lose all their material wealth as well, and their only offspring are mischief, trouble, and deceit. Here Eliphaz resorts to scare tactics. If Job won't accept the assumptions of the three friends, then perhaps he can be coerced to their point of view by this vividly lurid portrait of the fate of the wicked. In short, Eliphaz utterly rejects the possibility that Job may be right to raise questions. Such questioning is impiety that proves Job's wickedness.

Job responds first with an attack on the friends for not being friends. Had their roles been reversed, Job says, he would have given comfort and encouragement to them. These three, however, have harangued Job, they have wagged their heads and ground their teeth at him—signs of gloating and scornful hatred. They have, in fact, lied in accusing him of sinfulness. Especially hard to take is Eliphaz's charge of impiety. Job, guilty of impiety? Job describes his pitiful condition:

> My adversary sharpens his eyes against me.
> They have gaped at me with their mouths;
>> they have struck me insolently on the cheek;
>> they mass themselves together against me.
> God gives me up to the ungodly,

> and casts me into the hands of the wicked.
> I was at ease, and he broke me in two;
>   he seized me by the neck and dashed me to pieces;
> he set me up as his target;
>   his archers surround me.
> He slashes open my kidneys, and shows no mercy;
>   he pours out my gall on the ground.
> He bursts upon me again and again;
>   he rushes at me like a warrior.
> I have sewed sackcloth upon my skin,
>   and have laid my strength in the dust.
> My face is red with weeping,
>   and deep darkness in on my eyelids,
> though there is no violence in my hands,
>   and my prayer is pure. (16:9b-17)

The friends' attack on Job pales into insignificance when set beside God's attack on Job. God first leaves Job at the mercy of malefactors and the wicked. Then God sets upon Job, mauling him like a wild animal might, grabbing him by the neck and tossing him around. Job is God's target, arrows raining on him from every side. The arrows cut into Job's vital organs which spill onto the ground. God has utterly destroyed Job, so Job adopts the signs of grief and mourning—he dons sackcloth and rubs his forehead in the dirt. Graphically he describes his face as a contrast of red and black: the red from his flushed cheeks, the black from the circles around his eyes. But though in an attitude of mourning, he still asserts his innocence. He warns his friends not to mistake his mourning for an admission of guilt.

Since Job is on trial, since his integrity is in question, he calls on witnesses for his defense:

> O earth, do not cover my blood;
>   let my outcry find no resting place.
> Even now, in fact, my witness is in heaven,
>   and he that vouches for me is on high.
> My friends scorn me;
>   my eye pours out tears to God,
> that he would maintain the right of a mortal with God,
>   as one does for a neighbor.

For when a few years have come,
    I shall go the way from which I shall not return. (16:18-22)

Job has just described God's attack on him and now he identifies its exact nature: it is murder. God is murdering Job. So he cries for the earth not to cover his blood—that is, for the murder not to go undetected. The poet alludes here to the story of Cain and Abel. When Cain murdered Abel, God detected the murder because Abel's "blood is crying out to me from the ground" (Gen 4:10). God held Cain responsible for this unwarranted act of violence, and now Job accuses God of the same unwarranted act.

The idea of blood crying out from the earth suggests to Job the idea of a witness to his murder. In a moment of inspiration, he suddenly "sees" this witness who will testify for him, one "on high," one of the heavenly court surrounding God. This heavenly being is Job's assurance that his appeal will come before God. And when that appeal does come before God, Job believes he will be able once again to turn his eyes on God. In other words, the absence of God will be turned into the presence of God, Job's alienation will be overcome. Implicit in this hope is Job's assumption of innocence. Also implicit is his belief that God will be just and that when God hears Job's defense he will be exonerated and his suffering will cease. In spite of Job's harsh accusations of God's injustice, Job does not really want to believe that God is unjust. The logic of his circumstances has compelled him to consider this possibility. But his real desire is to find a reason why a just God would allow him to suffer, though he is innocent.

But this inspiration that there might be a heavenly defense counsel fades as quickly as it had come, because Job next, almost wistfully, expresses a wish for an arbitrator between him and God, one to listen to both sides and make a ruling. This desire is another assertion of innocence. If there *were* an arbitrator, the arbitrator would find in Job's favor. But who could arbitrate between God and a mortal? The idea is absurd almost, because no one could force God to do anything (as Job has already admitted). There is an urgency about Job's desire for exoneration because he will soon die, and then there will be no chance of justice.

There is only one who can really help Job, so Job's next appeal is to that one:

> My spirit is broken, my days are extinct,
>> the grave is ready for me.
> Surely there are mockers around me,
>> and my eye dwells on their provocation.
> Lay down a pledge for me with yourself;
>> who is there that will give surety for me?
> Since you have closed their minds to understanding,
>> therefore you will not let them triumph.
> Those who denounce friends for reward—
>> the eyes of their children will fail.
> He has made me a byword of the peoples,
>> and I am one before whom people spit.
> My eye had grown dim from grief,
>> and all my members are like a shadow.
> The upright are appalled at this,
>> and the innocent stir themselves up against the godless.
> Yet the righteous hold to their way,
>> and they that have clean hands grow stronger and stronger.
>> (17:1-9)

After his momentary burst of inspiration and hope, Job sinks back again into a feeling of hopelessness. Wherever he turns, he faces the taunts and sneers of others. So he appeals to God, the only direct address to God in the second cycle. If only God would vouch for him, for no one else will. If God *did* vouch for him, then those who taunt and sneer would not triumph over him. But even this possibility fades quickly away and Job sinks into a profound reverie on his ostracized state. In one last burst he challenges his friends:

> But you, come back now, all of you,
>> and I shall not find a sensible person among you. (17:10)

And then he strikes the last chords of his depression:

> My days are past, my plans are broken off,
>> the desires of my heart.

They make night into day;
  "The light," they say, "is near to the darkness."
If I look for Sheol as my house,
  if I spread my couch in darkness,
if I say to the Pit, "You are my father,"
  and to the worm, "My mother," or "My sister,"
where then is my hope?
  Who will see my hope?
Will it go down to the bars of Sheol?
  Shall we descend together into the dust? (17:11-16)

Job is utterly hopeless. His sudden inspiration about a witness or arbitrator has left him exhausted. He speaks in short, clipped phrases. His references to light and darkness, day and night, and to father and mother echo his curse in chapter three, but without the driving, forceful energy of anger he exhibited there. He cannot take his piety with him into Sheol. And when he does die, all hope will be gone.

Bildad and Job

Bildad is totally insensitive to Job's despair and takes Job's arguments as a personal affront. Job, he says, is treating the friends like dumb animals with no sense. Job, he says, wants the whole order of nature changed just to prove he is right. Bildad is indignant! Then he launches into a description of the wicked, parallel to Eliphaz's in chapter fifteen and vying with him in outrageous exaggeration. The light of the wicked dies down and fails (that is, their spirit, their life force), their iniquity causes their steps to totter, they rush headlong and unheedingly into every kind of trap and snare, disease eats them away, magicians cast evil spells over them, they leave no worthy reputation behind them, and their awful fate is fabled from east to west (that is, throughout the whole inhabited earth). Clearly Bildad means this description to apply to Job.

Bildad's cruelty is uncalled for, and we would expect Job to respond in kind. He has amply demonstrated his ability to give as well as take. But in his response to Bildad's second speech, Job demonstrates something else—his intellectual and moral superiority to his friends. He begins with an uncompromising statement of his innocence:

> How long will you torment me,
>   and break me in pieces with words?
> These ten times you have cast reproach upon me;
>   are you not ashamed to wrong me?
> And even if it is true that I have erred,
>   my error remains with me.
> If indeed you magnify yourselves against me,
>   and make my humiliation an argument against me,
> know then that God has put me in the wrong,
>   and closed his net around me.
> Even when I cry out, "Violence!" I am not answered;
>   I call aloud, but there is no justice.
> He has walled up my way so that I cannot pass,
>   and he has set darkness upon my paths.
> He has stripped my glory from me,
>   and taken the crown from my head.
> He breaks me down on every side, and I am gone,
>   he has uprooted my hope like a tree.
> He has kindled his wrath against me,
>   and counts me as his adversary.
> His troops come on together,
>   they have thrown up siegeworks against me,
>   and encamp around my tent. (19:2-12)

Job begins by trying to make his friends see what their attacks have done to him. They have exhausted him, they have pulverized him with words. Their words have not even been true. They have blamed him for his misfortunes, but the truth is that it is God who has done this to him, God who has put him in the wrong. Furthermore, they are failing ethically because Job has accused God of murder, but his friends refuse to consider his case. His friends will grant him no justice. Then Job elaborates his earlier theme regarding their failure in friendship:

> He has put my family far from me,
>   and my acquaintances are wholly estranged from me.

> My relatives and my close friends have failed me;
>> the guests in my house have forgotten me;
> my serving girls count me as a stranger;
>> I have become an alien in their eyes.
> I call to my servant, but he gives me no answer;
>> I must myself plead with him.
> My breath is repulsive to my wife;
>> I am loathsome to my own family.
> Even young children despise me;
>> when I rise, they talk against me.
> All my intimate friends abhor me,
>> and those whom I have loved have turned against me.
> My bones cling to my skin and to my flesh,
>> and I have escaped by the skin of my teeth. (19:13-20)

Job for the first time explicitly describes one more aspect of his suffering—being a social outcast. All classes of society reject him. Brothers, friends, kinspeople treat him as an alien or a stranger. His wife and family cannot bear his physical presence. Little children despise him with impunity. Then Job speaks words which are a high point of the dialogue:

> Have pity on me, have pity on me, O you my friends,
>> for the hand of God has touched me!
> Why do you, like God, pursue me,
>> never satisfied with my flesh?
> O that my words were written down!
>> O that they were inscribed in a book!
> O that with an iron pen and with lead
>> they were engraved on a rock forever!
> For I know that my Redeemer lives,
>> and that at the last he will stand upon the earth;
> and after my skin has been thus destroyed,
>> then in my flesh I shall see God,
> whom I shall see on my side,
>> and my eyes shall behold, and not another.
>> My heart faints within me! (19:21-27)

First we should notice Job's appeal to his friends for pity. In spite of the harsh words that have passed between them, he still values them and wants their friendship. Job should not be the one to have to make the overtures. He is the one who is suffering and needs understanding and compassion. One of the paradoxes of suffering, though, is that it can make the sufferer more open to others. And so, Job tries to overcome the barrier of ill will that has gone up between him and his friends by telling them what he wants from them. Furthermore, there is no need for them to pursue him or attack him. God's pursuit does quite an effective job by itself, and theirs is redundant.

Verses 25-27 are one of the most difficult passages of the book to interpret. The difficulties are manifold. First, the Hebrew text is so obscure that no two translations agree. Second, even if we accept one translation over another, the English meaning is not always apparent. Third, the familiarity of this passage—known to us as much through Handel's aria in *The Messiah* as through the Book of Job—causes a resistance to new translations. And finally, the familiar King James Version bolsters certain theological views about resurrection which make some of us resistant to alternative renderings. Scholars do agree that this translation is misleading and that a better translation is possible.

In verse 25 the NRSV uses the familiar word *redeemer*. This word means next of kin and can be translated, depending on context, as redeemer, avenger, or vindicator. Since in verse 25 Job declares his conviction that there is one who will vindicate or exonerate him, vindicator is probably the best translation. After I am dead, Job is saying, there will be one who will vindicate me. I may not have a written record, but I will have something even better, a living witness.

The remainder of this verse, however, is subject to some modification. "Last" is not adverbial, modifying the verb. Rather, it is adjectival, describing the vindicator. The vindicator is the last. This usage recalls Isaiah 44:6 and 48:12 where God is called the "first and the last." Verse 25 should therefore read: "But in my heart I know that my vindicator lives and that he, the Last, will stand upon the earth." This rendering means that Job is convinced that one day (after he is dead) someone will appear on earth to vindicate him. That someone is "the Last" who is then identified in the next verse as God.

Verse 26 is the most difficult of these verses. The Hebrew is unintelligible, and the English translations are consequently wildly variant and their meanings are uncertain. Any translation represents an educated guess. The NRSV means something like the following: On the day when Job's vindicator stands on earth Job will see him; in fact, Job will stand at the vindicator's side. And who is this defense attorney? It is God. *God* will defend Job, declare him innocent, clear his name. Ancient court procedure underlies this verse. The defendant stood in court between the accuser on the left and the defense counsel on the right. Job sees himself standing with God at his right hand taking the role of the defense. In his first response to Bildad, Job had tried out the idea of an arbitrator between God and himself. He mentioned it again in his response to Eliphaz in this cycle. The idea has now evolved into that of a vindicator who will not merely arbitrate but will exonerate. And the vindicator is God. Only God can ultimately justify both God and Job. Job's attitude is one of faith—that there is a moral order and that God guarantees it. Job clings desperately to that faith, for if there is no ultimate justification of human suffering, then the universe is irrational and absurd and morally chaotic.

In verse 27 Job reasserts his faith that he will see God and God will be at his side defending him. The question verses 26 and 27 raise is that of life after death. Is Job affirming belief in bodily resurrection? The context seems to imply that Job will be reembodied after his death in order to witness his vindication. If this is what the verses mean, then Job's thinking is all the more daring and creative. He has moved swiftly from the thought that he might be vindicated after death by a written record (which he would not witness), to the thought that he might be vindicated after death by a living witness (whom he will see). Probably Job speaks more than he understands.

We will probably never know exactly what these verses meant in the original manuscript. As we have them now in their poorly preserved state their general meaning seems to be an affirmation by Job that he will one day be exonerated though he doesn't know exactly how or when. As these verses now stand they are an affirmation of faith in a moral order guaranteed by God. And the poet makes this affirmation in spite of the evidence to the contrary.

Job's response to Bildad ends with a warning to the friends. If they impugn Job's innocence, then *they* are guilty of sin and judgment will fall upon them. Job's warning follows logically from his affirmation of the moral order in the immediately preceding verses. If innocent people like Job are exonerated eventually, then those guilty of sin will be held accountable eventually. Thus, the friends had better think carefully about what they say in accusing Job. Again Job is reaching out to his friends (as he did when he cried for their pity). You are my friends, Job declares, so be careful what you say. Don't say something you may be sorry for later.

Zophar and Job

Zophar's second speech indicates that he will not by swayed by Job's appeal to their friendship. Job's words distress Zophar and force him to reply. He, of course, does not state his own opinion, since human opinions are worthless, in his opinion. No, "a spirit beyond my understanding gives me the answers" (20:3b). Zophar thinks he can close off discussion by this appeal to supernatural knowledge. The fate of the wicked has been the same from the beginning of time down to the present. The wicked may prosper, but that prosperity is short-lived. "Though in his pride he stands high as the heavens, and his head touches the clouds, he will be swept utterly away like his own dung, and those used to seeing him will say, 'Where is he?'" (20:6-7). The triumph of the wicked is like a dream or vision in the night. One gets a glimpse of them but then they are gone. Though their evil tastes sweet in their mouth, it turns to poison in their stomach. They cannot digest the fruit of their ill-gotten prosperity, for God makes them vomit it back up. Then Zophar declares:

> God will send his fierce anger into them,
>   and rain it upon them as their food.
> They will flee from an iron weapon;
>   a bronze arrow will strike them through.
> It is drawn forth and comes out of their body,
>   and the glittering point comes out of their gall. (20:23b-25a)

Zophar nowhere says that this is a description of Job, but this passage contains unmistakable allusions to Job's self-description in 16:12-14. So Zophar is really saying that Job has condemned himself as wicked. For Job to admit that God's arrows are aimed at him and that God's attack has spilled his gall is for him to admit that he is guilty.

Job had appealed to his friends' pity in responding the second time to Bildad. At the beginning of his response to Zophar, he attempts once more to rouse their sympathy:

> Listen carefully to my words,
>   and let this be your consolation.
> Bear with me, and I will speak;
>   then after I have spoken, mock on.
> As for me, is my complaint addressed to mortals?
>   Why should I not be impatient?
> Look at me, and be appalled,
>   and lay your hand upon your mouth.
> When I think of it I am dismayed,
>   and shuddering seizes my flesh. (21:2-6)

If the friends cannot really feel sympathy, then at least they can listen in silence. That would be some comfort to Job. Just looking at Job should be sufficient to silence them. When he thinks about his plight, he is horrified and convulsed.

Job had defended himself by appealing to his unblemished life. Now he broadens his argument by showing that the facts refute his friends' assertions that the wicked always suffer for their wickedness. Zophar had said that the prosperity of the wicked passes quickly away. Job explicitly denies this:

> Why do the wicked live on,
>   reach old age, and grow mighty in power?
> Their children are established in their presence,
>   and their offspring before their eyes.
> Their houses are safe from fear,
>   and no rod of God is upon them.
> Their bull breeds without fail;
>   their cow calves and never miscarries.
> They send out their little ones like a flock,

and their children dance around.
They sing to the tambourine and the lyre,
    and rejoice to the sound of the pipe.
They spend their days in prosperity,
    and in peace they go down to Sheol.
They say to God, "Leave us alone!
    We do not desire to know your ways.
What is the Almighty, that we should serve him?
    And what profit do we get if we pray to him?" (21:7-15)

Just look at the facts, Job says. The fact is that the wicked often are not punished for their sins. Their prosperity is not fleeting, as Zophar had said. Their whole lives are filled with the good things of life so that they can go down to Sheol in peace. And all of this is true even though they snub God and ignore God's will.

Job follows this passage with a series of rhetorical questions which reinforce his point. Then, in the midst of these questions, he considers a possible defense the friends might fall back on, if they admit the evidence he has presented. They might say that God will punish the children of the wicked, if not the wicked themselves. But Job rejects this. The wicked are to be "paid in full and be punished" (21:19b). Job reflects here a growing awareness of individual responsibility. This was an idea first explicitly stated by Jeremiah some time prior to the Exile (Jer 31:21-30). Jeremiah's brief statement of individual responsibility was then picked up by Ezekiel and given a full commentary in the first part of the Exile. (All of Ezekiel 18 is a detailed gloss on the original idea of individual responsibility.) Job sees the injustice of punishing someone for the sins of someone else. And since he wants to find a God of justice, he asserts individual responsibility.

Yet, the facts of human experience seem to be against him. There seems to be no justice in this life. The wicked not only prosper, they actually are honored. So Job concludes: "How then will you comfort me with empty nothings? There is nothing left of your answers but falsehood" (21:34).

And on that note the second cycle of speeches ends.

Chapter 5

The Third Cycle and the Speeches of Elihu

The pattern of the dialogue breaks down irretrievably in the third cycle of speeches. Only Eliphaz's speech and Job's response remain intact. The speech attributed to Bildad has been abbreviated to only six verses (including the introductory formula). The responses to Bildad attributed to Job are diametrically contrary to what he had previously asserted. Both Zophar's third speech and Job's response are missing—at least neither is identified as such. It seems unlikely that the poet deliberately broke the pattern established in the first two cycles. And it seems unlikely that the poet suddenly had Job change his mind about the main point of contention. It is more likely that a later editor, shocked perhaps at Job's flouting of the orthodox view, rearranged the text of the third cycle so that Job finally sounds right.

The Third Cycle

We will examine the text of the third cycle as we now have it and suggest some possible reconstructions. Eliphaz begins this cycle with an accusation of specific, damning crimes against Job:

> Can a mortal be of use to God?
>> Can even the wisest be of service to him?
> Is it any pleasure to the Almighty if you are righteous,
>> or is it gain to him if you make your ways blameless?

Is it for your piety that he reproves you,
　and enters into judgment with you?
Is not your wickedness great?
　There is no end to your iniquities.
For you have exacted pledges from your family for no reason,
　and stripped the naked of their clothing.
You have given no water to the weary to drink,
　and you have withheld bread from the hungry.
The powerful possess the land,
　and the favored live in it.
You have sent widows away empty-handed,
　and the arms of the orphans you have crushed.
Therefore snares are around you,
　and sudden terror overwhelms you,
or darkness so that you cannot see;
　a flood of water covers you.
Is not God high in the heavens?
　See the highest stars, how lofty they are!
Therefore you say, "What does God know?
　Can he judge through the deep darkness?
Thick clouds enwrap him, so that he does not see,
　and he walks on the dome of heaven."
Will you keep to the old way
　that the wicked have trod?
They were snatched away before their time,
　their foundation was washed away by a flood.
They said to God, "Leave us alone,"
　and "What can the Almighty do to us?"
Yet he filled their houses with good things—
　but the plans of the wicked are repugnant to me.
The righteous see it and are glad;
　the innocent laugh them to scorn,
saying, "Surely our adversaries are cut off,
　and what they left, the fire has consumed." (22:2-20)

The friends had implied Job's sinfulness in their earlier speeches,
and Job had challenged Eliphaz in the first cycle to be specific. In
this cycle Eliphaz *is* specific. His charges against Job are two-fold.
First, Job is utterly depraved and immoral. He has foreclosed contracts without due cause, refused to come to the aid of the helpless and deprived, rejected the pleas of widows and orphans.

Second, Job is an "atheist." "Atheism" is a term never found in the Hebrew Bible, and it may be misleading to use it here. An atheist is one who denies God. But there are two ways that may happen. In the modern sense it means one who denies God's existence, one who says there is no God. In the Hebrew Bible, however, the atheist is the one who lives and acts *as if* God did not exist. God may exist as a real being, but that existence makes no practical difference. It is this kind of atheism with which Eliphaz indicts Job.

We should not take these charges too seriously. Job was renowned for his righteousness. In the Prologue he is presented as perhaps overly scrupulous about what God thinks. Though the Job of the Prologue and the Job of the poetry are two different persons, they are not different in that one is righteous and the other sinful. How then should we interpret these charges? It appears that Eliphaz has forged these accusations in the heat of his righteous indignation. It is so palpably clear to him that Job *must* be a sinner, and Job's suffering is so undeniably great, that Eliphaz logically concludes that Job's sins are the very worst possible. He knows a priori that Job must be guilty of these sins, though a posteriori he has no reason to believe this.

Job does not dignify Eliphaz's accusations by a direct response. Rather, he meditates once again on the possibility of stating his case before God:

> Today also my complaint is bitter;
>> his hand is heavy despite my groaning.
> Oh, that I knew where I might find him,
>> that I might come even to his dwelling!
> I would lay my case before him,
>> and fill my mouth with arguments.
> I would learn what he would answer me,
>> and understand what he would say to me.
> Would he contend with me in the greatness of his power?
>> No; but he would give heed to me.
> There an upright person could reason with him,
>> and I should be acquitted forever by my judge.
> If I go forward, he is not there;
>> or backward, I cannot perceive him;
> on the left he hides, and I cannot behold him;
>> I turn to the right, but I cannot see him. (23:2-9)

The paradox of Job's suffering is that in one sense God is very much a presence in his life but in another sense God is absent. Job feels God's presence in his sufferings—they are the heavy hand of God on him. But Job feels God's absence in his frustrated longing for an explanation from God. If Job could ever enter the presence of God, then he could find out whatever it is God would say. Furthermore, if he could ever enter the presence of God, he would be vindicated because God vindicates the upright. (Job alludes here to his response to Bildad in the second cycle.) But no matter where Job turns, he cannot find God. He looks east and west, north and south but can never catch a glimpse of God. Job whirls in every direction, but God is an elusive presence who refuses to be known.

Though Job cannot find God, God certainly has found Job:

> But he knows the way that I take;
> >   when he has tested me, I shall come out like gold.
> My foot has held fast to his steps;
> >   I have kept his way and have not turned aside.
> I have not departed from the commandment of his lips;
> >   I have treasured in my bosom the words of his mouth.
> But he stands alone and who can dissuade him?
> >   What he desires, that he does.
> For he will complete what he appoints for me;
> >   and many such things are in his mind.
> Therefore I am terrified at his presence;
> >   when I consider, I am in dread of him.
> God has made my heart faint;
> >   the Almighty has terrified me;
> If only I could vanish in darkness,
> >   and thick darkness would cover my face! (23:10-17)

Job now answers the charges levelled by Eliphaz. *God* knows that Job is righteous (even if Eliphaz does not: "Receive instruction from his mouth, and lay up his words in your heart," 22:22). God knows that Job has kept to the right path, followed God's commands, stored in his heart what God says. But even though Job has faithfully kept God's word, he does not claim to know the mind of God. God's actions are full of divine purpose, and no mortal can hope to know what those purposes are. Thus, though Job has insisted on meeting God, he is afraid. Who can know the outcome of such a meeting? Nevertheless, Job will not be reduced to silence by the awful mystery of God. He still hopes for a confrontation which will exonerate him.

The problems in the third cycle begin to appear in full force in chapter 24. Job is still speaking in response to Eliphaz. The first half of this speech draws a contrast between the wicked and those they oppress. But in verse 18 Job denounces the wicked and proclaims that God will surely punish them. This flatly contradicts his response to Zophar in the second cycle where he asserted that the wicked often go unpunished. It seems likely, therefore, that 24:18-25 should be attributed to one of the friends, not Job. Some scholars suggest that these verses may be part of Zophar's missing speech and should be connected with 27:11-23.

Chapter 25 presents us with the next problem. It totals six verses (and one of them is the formula for introduction, "Then Bildad the Shuhite answered . . ."). This speech is, therefore, actually only five verses long and gives the impression of being the middle part of a speech whose beginning and end are missing. Since the speeches have averaged twenty-nine verses in length, the presumption is that part of this one is missing. There is reason to believe that part of the missing speech is found in 26:5-14. These verses do not follow coherently from Job's opening response (which accuses Bildad of failing as a friend). Also, chapter 27 begins, "Job again took up his discourse. . . ." A subsequent editor has apparently interpreted 26:5-14 as an interruption of Job's response to Bildad. If so, then this response probably consisted of 26:2-4 and 27:2-10.

Finally, we must ask what happened to the third speech of Zophar and Job's response? A partial solution would be to attribute 27:11-23 to Zophar, verses now found in Job's response to Bildad but inconsistent with everything Job has said so far. They are yet another description of the terrible lot God prescribes for the wicked, parallel to the arguments all three friends employed in the second cycle. It is unlikely that Job would suddenly change his mind and agree with the friends that the wicked are always punished. So, it is reasonable to attribute these verses to one of the friends and specifically to Zophar, since his last speech is missing.

What about Job's missing response to Zophar? Assuming the above reconstruction, we might be tempted to take chapter 28 as Job's answer. It follows our reconstruction of Zophar's speech and is, in the present text, attributed to Job. It is a meditation on the mystery of finding wisdom, structured according to one large antithetical parallelism. The first eleven verses describe the marvelous way miners burrow into the earth to extract precious metals and gems. With great and difficult work we can extract hidden treasures. But what sort of mining operation can ever get the ore of wisdom? Verses 12-28 play on the inability of human beings to ever discover wisdom through their own ingenuity. It concludes with the standard advice of the sage: "The fear of the Lord, that is wisdom; and to depart from evil is understanding" (28:28).

The tone of this poem is certainly unlike anything Job has thus far said. It is calm, meditative, quiet, full of wonder at the mystery of wisdom. Job's speeches have, in contrast, been passionate, rising full of hope one moment and plunging full of despair the next. In fact, Job has rejected the wisdom of his friends, and it is here inconsistent for him to become a proponent of wisdom. Furthermore, chapter 29 begins with the formula, "Job again took up his discourse," which again probably indicates that a later editor recognized chapter 28 as an interruption. I think we must conclude that Job's response to Zophar is simply missing. We do not know who authored chapter 28.

All of the foregoing is hypothetical. Without new evidence, we will never know the solution to these problems. It is also hazardous trying to interpret these passages, since we cannot be sure who is saying what. It is not satisfying to have all this ambiguity regarding the third cycle, but we must be agnostic regarding the positions taken by Job, Bildad, and Zophar. We do not know what further developments may have occurred in Job's thought.

We can, however, summarize what Job has said up to this point of textual disruption. First, he denies the basic assumption of the friends that only the wicked suffer, and its corollary that since he is suffering he must be wicked. The facts are that the wicked often prosper and "go down to Sheol in peace." Second, he resolutely maintains his innocence of any wrongdoing which would justify his suffering. He is not suffering because God is punishing him for some sin. And third, he resolutely holds out the hope that somewhere, somehow, he will know the reasons for his suffering.

Job's Final Defense

There is nothing more for the friends to say to Job or for Job to say to his friends. The dialogue is over. They are at an impasse. Job's lively consideration of daring new possibilities contrasts sharply with the increasingly rigid orthodoxy of his friends. Job, therefore, brings the dialogue to a close with a stunning peroration. In chapter 29 he reviews his past good fortune, beginning with his wistful cry, "Oh, that I were as in the months of old, as in the days when God watched over me" (29:2). In those old days he had the respect of his peers, who "laid their hands on their mouths" (29:9) and kept silence when he spoke. His peers do that now, too, but in horror, not respect. Job was spoken of with favor, his reputation above reproach. Because of this he believed that he would live to a ripe old age, his powers unimpaired, his life still vigorous.

In chapter 30 he makes the transition to his present plight: "But now they make sport of me" (30:1), and by people he would have taken no notice of earlier, by the very lowest and vilest social classes. Now when he calls for help, God does not answer:

> I cry to you and you do not answer me,
> I stand, and you merely look at me.
> You have turned cruel to me;
> with the might of your hand you persecute me.
> You lift me up on the wind, you make me ride on it,
> and you toss me about in the roar of the storm.
> I know that you will bring me to death,
> and to the house appointed for all living. (30:20-23)

Nevertheless, Job proclaims his innocence and the injustice of his suffering.

He ends with a mighty oath of clearance, his final challenge to God to appear and explain his suffering.

If my step has turned aside from the way,
>   and my heart has followed my eyes,
>   and if any spot has clung to my hands;
then let me sow, and another eat;
>   and let what grows for me be rooted out.
If my heart has been enticed by a woman,
>   and I have lain in wait at my neighbor's door;
then let my wife grind for another,
>   and let other men kneel over her. . . .
If I have rejected the cause of my male or female slaves,
>   when they brought a complaint against me;
what then shall I do when God rises up?
>   When he makes inquiry, what shall I answer him? . . .
If I have withheld anything that the poor desired,
>   or have caused the eyes of the widow to fail,
or have eaten my morsel alone,
>   and the orphan has not eaten from it—
for from my youth I reared the orphan like a father,
>   and from my mother's womb I guided the widow—
if I have seen anyone perish for lack of clothing,
>   or a poor person without covering,
whose loins have not blessed me,
>   and who was not warmed with the fleece of my sheep,
if I have raised my hand against the orphan,
>   because I saw I had supporters at the gate;
then let my shoulder blade fall from my shoulder,
>   and let my arm be broken from its socket.
For I was in terror of calamity from God,
>   and I could not have faced his majesty.
If I have made gold my trust,
>   or called fine gold my confidence;
if I have rejoiced because my wealth was great,
>   or because my hand had gotten much;
if I have looked at the sun when it shone,
>   or the moon moving in splendor,
and my heart has been secretly enticed,
>   and my mouth has kissed my hand;
this also would be an iniquity to be punished by the judges,
>   for I should have been false to God above. . . .
If my land has cried out against me,
>   and its furrows have wept together;

> if I have eaten its yield without payment,
>   and caused the death of its owners;
> let thorns grow instead of wheat,
>   and foul weeds instead of barley. (31:7-10, 13-14, 16-28, 38-40)

These words are as strong as any Job has declared to argue his innocence. "If I have been guilty of this offense, then may I suffer this curse," he declares. In each case, the curse fits the sin. The first curse has to do with covetousness. If he has coveted anything of his neighbor's (including his neighbor's wife), then may his own property (including his own wife) be forfeited. The second curse has to do with his treatment of those less fortunate than he. If he has refused alms to those in need, or if he has used his social influence to steal from the poor, knowing that the judges who are his friend will find in his favor, then may he lose that influence and power. (To treat the poor and the powerless this way would be to raise his arm against them. To have his arm wrenched out of its socket would be to render him unable to raise his arm in injustice. The poet may have Nathan's parable to King David in mind, 2 Sam 12:1-14.)

The third curse concerns idolatry—toward either material goods or some natural object like the sun. To worship an idol instead of the true God would be an offense against the Law and unfaithfulness to God. In Deuteronomy 29:16-29 we find a summary of all the curses that flow from idolatry. The final curse listed has to do with the dishonest use of land or others' resources without paying recompense. The curse is that this fruitfulness will cease.

To the Hebrew mind, speaking the word was almost the same as creating the reality. Thus, Job is declaring as strongly as possible by these oaths that he is innocent. If he is guilty of the terrible deeds described in each "if" clause, then he is virtually assuring the reality of each "then" clause.

Finally, in one last desperate cry, Job finishes:

> Oh, that I had one to hear me!
>   (Here is my signature! let the Almighty answer me!)
>   Oh, that I had the indictment written by my adversary!
> Surely I would carry it on my shoulder;

> I would bind it on me like a crown;
> I would give him an account of all my steps;
>   like a prince I would approach him. (31:35-37)

Job's integrity has been called into question and his only defense is "an account of all my steps," the whole record of his life.

The Speeches of Elihu

Job has silenced his friends with his final defense. And his oath of clearance is a direct challenge to God. That is, the oath declares his innocence in the strongest possible terms. He has nothing else to say, and if something more *is* to be said it will have to come from God. God's speeches probably began at this point in the original poem. In our present text, however, a fifth speaker suddenly appears and launches into the longest continuous speech in the poem, then disappears without a trace. The speaker's name is Elihu, and he is younger than the others. He offers his youth as his reason for having remained silent till now. Finally, though, he speaks because none of the other friends had refuted or silenced Job. Besides, he reasons that age by itself is no guarantee of wisdom, that wisdom comes from the spirit of God. It is God who will refute Job, not a mere mortal. Nevertheless, Elihu, a mere mortal, is just bursting to speak. He asserts—with no apparent consciousness of irony—that he will be ruthlessly honest, flattering neither God nor his fellows. There is probably no better portrait of impetuous, idealistic, and ignorant youth than Elihu. At the beginning of his speech, for example, he asserts, "My words declare the uprightness of my heart, and what my lips know they speak sincerely" (33:3). And toward the end he says, "For truly my words are not false" (36:4). He is certain of his own rightness. He is eager to show up his elders because they have failed to make Job repent. And so, after a whole chapter of introductory remarks, he finally gets around to launching his main theme—the absolute sovereignty of a gracious God.

Before examining the content of these speeches, we need to explore their function. On the face of it they are an interruption to the ordered progression of the poetry. The argument has reached an impasse that only the appearance of God can resolve.

Job's oath of clearance is a direct challenge to God and prepares dramatically for God's appearance. Instead of God, however, we get Elihu. It seems clear that from a literary point of view chapters 32–37 were added later and were not original to the poem. We need not detain ourselves with the question of who may have written these chapters, but we can discern a reason why they were added. First, Elihu's speeches deepen the dramatic tension by delaying God's long-awaited appearance. God's speeches, when they do come, are therefore all the more effective. Second, Elihu's descriptions of nature foreshadow some of the themes of God's speeches. And, finally, Elihu's vivid, graphic description of the thunderstorm which ends his last speech is the most effective introduction imaginable for the God who speaks out of the storm.

In content, these speeches actually add a new concept. Elihu's point of view is essentially that of the three friends—sinners suffer, the righteous prosper. He differs, however, in his concept of God's purpose in causing the sinner to suffer. Suffering is a sign of God's grace, of God's gracious attempts to turn the sinner back to righteousness:

> In a dream, in a vision of the night,
>   when deep sleep falls on mortals,
>   while they slumber on their beds,
> then he opens their ears,
>   and terrifies them with warnings,
> that he may turn them aside from their deeds,
>   and keep them from pride,
> to spare their souls from the Pit,
>   their lives from traversing the River.
> They are also chastened with pain upon their beds,
>   and with continual strife in their bones.
> so that their lives loathe bread,
>   and their appetites dainty food.
> Their flesh is so wasted away that it cannot be seen;
>   and their bones, once invisible, now stick out.
> Their souls draw near the Pit,
>   and their lives to those who bring death.
> Then, if there should be for one of them an angel,
>   a mediator, one of a thousand,
>   one who declares a person upright,

and he is gracious to that person, and says,
"Deliver him from going down into the Pit;
    I have found a ransom;
let his flesh become fresh with youth;
    let him return to the days of his youthful vigor."
Then he prays to God, and is accepted by him,
    he comes into his presence with joy,
and God repays him for his righteousness.
    That person sings to others and says,
"I sinned, and perverted what was right,
    and it was not paid back to me.
He has redeemed my soul from going down to the Pit,
    and my life shall see the light."
God indeed does all these things,
    twice, three times, with mortals,
to bring back their souls from the Pit,
    so that they may see the light of life. (33:15-30)

Elihu believes that suffering can bring us back to God, so he chronicles the dangers of human existence. Accidents and disease bring us close to death, and the only thing that saves us is that God snatches us from the brink of the pit (that is, from descending into Sheol). The purpose of this last minute rescue is to give us a chance to confess our sin which brought us to the brink in the first place. God delivers us again and again so that we may enjoy the full light of life. A new idea has been interjected: that suffering is not mere punishment but is also redemptive.

Elihu's other contribution is a towering conception of the absolute sovereignty of God:

Surely, you have spoken in my hearing,
    and I have heard the sound of your words.
You say, "I am clean, without transgression;
    I am pure, and there is no iniquity in me.
Look, he finds occasions against me,
    he counts me as his enemy;
he puts my feet in the stocks,
    and watches all my paths."

But in this you are not right. I will answer you:
    God is greater than any mortal.

> Why do you contend against him,
>> saying, "He will answer one of my words"?
> For God speaks in one way,
>> and in two, though people do not perceive it. (33:8-14)

The very idea of Job contending with God is wrongheaded. God is so much greater than we are that it is useless to do so. Not even the most powerful human beings—princes, politicians, the rich—have any power with God.

> If you have understanding, hear this;
>> listen to what I say.
> Shall one who hates justice govern?
>> Will you condemn one who is righteous and mighty,
> who says to a king, "You scoundrel!"
>> and to princes, "You wicked men!";
> who shows no partiality to nobles,
>> nor regards the rich more than the poor,
>> for they are all the work of his hands?
> In a moment they die;
>> at midnight the people are shaken and pass away,
>> and the mighty are taken away by no human hand.
> For his eyes are upon the ways of mortals,
>> and he sees all their steps.
> There is no gloom or deep darkness
>> where evildoers may hide themselves.
> For he has not appointed a time for anyone
>> to go before God in judgment.
> He shatters the mighty without investigation,
>> and sets others in their place.
> Thus, knowing their works,
>> he overturns them in the night, and they are crushed.
> He strikes them for their wickedness
>> while others look on,
>> because they turned aside from following him,
>> and had no regard for any of his ways,
>> so that they caused the cry of the poor to come to him,
>> and he heard the cry of the afflicted. . . . (34:16-28)

Even nations, which outlive individuals, cannot stand before this sovereign God.

This concept of God's absolute sovereignty culminates in Elihu's description of God as the God of the thunderstorm:

> Can anyone understand the spreading of the clouds,
>   the thunderings of his pavilion?
> See, he scatters his lightning around him
>   and covers the roots of the sea.
> For by these he governs peoples;
>   he gives food in abundance.
> He covers his hands with the lightning,
>   and commands it to strike the mark.
> Its crashing tells about him;
>   he is jealous with anger against iniquity.
> At this also my heart trembles,
>   and leaps out of its place.
> Listen, listen to the thunder of his voice
>   and the rumbling that comes from his mouth.
> Under the whole heaven he lets it loose,
>   and his lightning to the corners of the earth.
> After it his voice roars;
>   he thunders with his majestic voice
>   and he does not restrain the lightnings
>   when his voice is heard. (36:29–37:4)

This is a powerful description of the thunderstorm as the voice of God. Elihu continues:

> Then the animals go into their lairs
>   and remain in their dens.
> From its chamber comes the whirlwind,
>   and cold from the scattering winds.
> By the breath of God ice is given,
>   and the broad waters are frozen fast.
> He loads the thick cloud with moisture;
>   the clouds scatter his lightning.
> They turn round and round by his guidance,
>   to accomplish all that he commands them
>   on the face of the habitable world.
> Whether for correction, or for his land,
>   or for love, he causes it to happen.
> Hear this, O Job;
>   stop and consider the wondrous works of God.

Do you know how God lays his command upon them,
    and causes the lightning of his cloud to shine?
Do you know the balancings of the clouds,
    the wondrous works of the one whose knowledge is perfect,
you whose garments are hot
    when the earth is still because of the south wind?
Can you, like him, spread out the skies,
    hard as a molten mirror? . . .
Now, no one can look on the light
    when it is bright in the skies,
    when the wind has passed and cleared them.
Out of the north comes golden splendor;
    around God is awesome majesty.
The Almighty—we cannot find him;
    he is great in power and justice,
    and abundant righteousness he will not violate.
Therefore mortals fear him;
    he does not regard any who are wise in their own conceit.
    (37:9-18, 21-24)

The God whose absence is one source of Job's suffering is a God who is present indirectly in the mighty works of nature such as the thunderstorm. As Elihu describes the storm, a real storm begins to brew on the horizon and move toward Job and his friends. As the storm breaks in all its fury, God at long last appears and speaks.

Chapter 6

The Presence of God

Let us picture the scene before us. Job sits on the refuse heap, his friends seated silently around him. Elihu has finished speaking, his oration having climaxed with the vivid imagery of the storm. As he has spoken, the sky has grown dark. Lightning flashes on the horizon, and a low peal of thunder rumbles toward them. Dark clouds roll in from the west like an invading army. Though daytime, they are astonished by a darkness like that of night. A cold wind rushes past, chilling their sweaty bodies, relieving the sultry heat of the summer day.

God's First Speech

The storm breaks, and out of its fury God finally speaks:

> Who is this that darkens counsel by words
>   without knowledge?
> Gird up your loins like a man,
>   I will question you, and you shall declare to me. (38:2-3)

After Elihu's profuse pomposity, God's clean, direct, unambiguous speech stands out in sharp contrast. Elihu could only describe the storm: God is the reality itself. God's speech cleanses the atmosphere of the dialogue like a mighty summer storm cleanses a sultry day.

The identification of God with the storm is common in the Hebrew Bible. When Moses received the Law (Exod 19–20) dark clouds covered Mount Sinai, lightning flashed, and God spoke out of the thunder. Ezekiel, the first prophet of the Exile, received his call to be a prophet with a vision of a storm which contained the divine presence (Ezek 1:4). In the storm, the Hebrew people saw the presence of a majestic but terrifying God. The storm is the occasion of God's self-revelation. So out of the storm God speaks directly to Job. (The question in verse 2 clearly refers to Job, not Elihu—another indication that God's speeches originally followed directly upon Job's final defense.) God then announces the theme of these speeches: Job's ignorance of God's design. This is why God is at long last appearing: to show that Job has failed to see the divine purpose.

But something else is happening in these speeches, something only hinted at here. God is going to vindicate Job. Thus, God commands Job to "brace" himself, to "stand up like a man," to prepare to answer questions. The usual translation of "brace yourself" is "gird up your loins." The lower portion of the garment worn by males would be hitched up and tucked into the waist-band or belt (the girdle) to make possible greater freedom of movement. "Girding your loins" thus became a symbol for preparing for some difficult or dangerous task, such as going into battle. Some commentators believe that this may be an oblique reference to belt wrestling (in which points were scored by holds on the belt rather than falls) and that such wrestling may have been a Hebrew court procedure. In any case, God is challenging Job to defend himself. Job is to stand up, face God directly, and answer God's questions. In other words, God recognizes Job as a person, one who can be questioned and be held responsible for word and deed. God's direct address to Job affirms Job's dignity and honors him.

Then begins a series of mighty rhetorical questions:

> Where were you when I laid the foundation of the earth?
>   Tell me, if you have understanding.
> Who determined its measurements—surely you know!
>   Or who stretched the line upon it?
> On what were its bases sunk,
>   or who laid its cornerstone
> when the morning stars sang together

and all the heavenly beings shouted for joy?
Or who shut in the sea with doors
    when it burst out from the womb?—
when I made the clouds its garment,
    and thick darkness its swaddling band,
and prescribed bounds for it,
    and set bars and doors,
and said, "Thus far shall you come, and no farther,
    and here shall your proud waves be stopped"? (38:4-11)

These are magnificent questions. They break over us, wave after wave, like the gusting sheets of rain in a summer thunderstorm. They build up, piling one on top of another, like the massive, dark clouds of a summer tempest. God is the creator of the earth and sea. Does Job understand how this was done? God built the earth like mortals build a building, determining its dimensions and measuring it out. God secures the supporting pillars of the earth (does Job know on what these pillars rest?) and sets the earth's cornerstone in place. When mortals lay a foundation, they celebrate with song. So, when God laid the foundation of the earth, the stars sang together in concert and the heavenly host shouted their praise. Does Job understand the mysteries of the sea over whose birth God presided like a midwife? The imagery of the sea is graphic. Water bursts from the womb, and the newborn infant is wrapped in a blanket of cloud and cradled in fog. Then the image changes. God establishes the physical boundaries of the sea, its walls and doors. The sea symbolized chaos—everything that threatened God's creations, all the forces opposed to God. But God controls the sea and will not let it get out of bounds. Does Job comprehend how this was done?

God is also the creator of day and night:

Have you commanded the morning since your days began,
    and caused the dawn to know its place,
so that it might take hold of the skirts of the earth,
    and the wicked be shaken out of it?
It is changed like clay under the seal,
    and it is dyed like a garment.
Light is withheld from the wicked,
    and their uplifted arm is broken.

> Have you entered into the springs of the sea,
> > or walked in the recesses of the deep?
> Have the gates of death been revealed to you,
> > or have you seen the gates of deep darkness?
> Have you comprehended the expanse of the earth?
> > Declare, if you know all of this.
> Where is the way to the dwelling of light,
> > and where is the place of darkness,
> that you may take it to its territory
> > and that you may discern the paths to its home?
> Surely you know, for you were born then,
> > and the number of your days is great! (38:12-21)

Does Job understand the mysteries of night and day, light and dark? Can he explain this most regular of natural phenomena? God likens the darkness of night to a blanket spread over the earth. Dawn grasps the edges of the blanket and peels it back, light flooding from the sky from the horizon to the zenith. As morning comes, the horizon—whose features are indistinguishable in the blackness of night—takes on form like a smooth, wet clay tablet does under a seal. Has Job explored the world in its vastness, from the depths of the earth where darkness dwells to the home of the light? Of course he has not, and God makes that point abundantly clear with the sarcasm of verse 21.

This natural order of day and night reflects another, more significant order—the moral order of right and wrong—as symbolized by the coming of the dawn (verses 13-15). It is under the cover of darkness that the wicked do their evil deeds, thinking that no one (including God) will see them. The spreading light of dawn causes the wicked to scurry around seeking some place where the light will not penetrate, else the light of day will expose their evil. Verse 15 changes the image. The coming of light breaks the uplifted arm of the wicked—uplifted to do evil. The light of day, in threatening the exposure of the wicked, stops evil as surely as breaking the arm of the wicked would. God has established a natural order which reflects the moral order. These verses are an indirect answer to Job's question about the justice of suffering. Though Job has questioned it, there *is* a moral order, and the orderly sequence of day and night is a reflection of that order.

God, creator of earth and sea, the maker of day and night, is also the controller of all heavenly phenomena:

> Have you entered the storehouses of the snow,
> > or have you seen the storehouses of the hail,
> which I have reserved for the time of trouble,
> > for the day of battle and war?
> What is the way to the place where the light is distributed,
> > or where the east wind is scattered upon the earth?
> Who has cut a channel for the torrents of rain,
> > and a way for the thunderbolt,
> to bring rain on a land where no one lives,
> > on the desert, which is empty of human life,
> to satisfy the waste and desolate land,
> > and to make the ground put forth grass?
> Has the rain a father,
> > or who has begotten the drops of dew?
> From whose womb did the ice come forth,
> > and who has given birth to the hoarfrost of heaven?
> The waters become hard like stone,
> > and the face of the deep is frozen.
> Can you bind the chains of the Pleiades,
> > or loose the cords of Orion?
> Can you lead forth the Mazzaroth in their season,
> > or can you guide the Bear with its children?
> Do you know the ordinances of the heavens?
> > Can you establish their rule on the earth?
> Can you lift up your voice to the clouds,
> > so that a flood of waters may cover you?
> Can you send forth lightnings, so that they may go
> > and say to you, "Here we are"?
> Who has put wisdom in the inwards parts,
> > or given understanding to the mind?
> Who has the wisdom to number the clouds?
> > Or who can tilt the waterskins of the heavens,
> when the dust runs into a mass
> > and the clods cling together? (38:22-38)

This is a magnificent conception of the created order (and a compendium of ancient cosmology). God pictures the heavens as a vast structure towering over the earth, full of storehouses, arsenals, and cisterns for the heavenly phenomena that do God's bidding on earth—snow and hail, heat and wind, the rain. Who can comprehend the mysteries of water which falls as rain inexplicably on the uninhabited wilderness turning it green with growth or which, even more inexplicably, sometimes becomes hardened like stone when it freezes? Who controls the ordered progression of the stars as the signs of the zodiac rise, each in its appointed season? Can Job command the lightning and rain as God does? No, of course not. Job does not understand these things, much less control them. Who, then, is he to have challenged God who does control and understand?

We are dazzled by this poetic brilliance. But the poet has hardly begun. God turns from the physical universe with its wonders to the mysteries of living things:

> Can you hunt the prey for the lion,
>   or satisfy the appetite of the young lions,
> when they crouch in their dens,
>   or lie in wait in their covert?
> Who provides for the raven its prey,
>   when its young ones cry to God,
>   and wander about for lack of food?
> Do you know when the mountain goats give birth?
>   Do you observe the calving of the deer?
> Can you number the months that they fulfill,
>   and do you know the time when they give birth,
> when they crouch to give birth to their offspring,
>   and are delivered of their young?
> Their young ones become strong, they grow up in the open;
>   they go forth, and do not return to them.
> Who has let the wild ass go free?
>   Who has loosed the bonds of the swift ass,
> to which I have given the steppe for its home,
>   the salt land for its dwelling place?
> It scorns the tumult of the city;
>   it does not hear the shouts of the driver.
> It ranges the mountains as its pasture,
>   and it searches after every green thing.
> Is the wild ox willing to serve you?
>   Will it spend the night at your crib?

Can you tie it in the furrow with ropes,
  or will it harrow the valleys after you?
Will you depend on it because its strength is great,
  and will you hand over your labor to it?
Do you have faith in it that it will return,
  and bring your grain to your threshing floor? (38:39–39:12)

If Job does not understand the wonders of the physical universe, then perhaps he understands the ways of living things. What about the most common of daily activities, finding food to sustain life? What about the single most important function of living things, the reproduction of their kind? Does Job understand these most basic functions? Does he understand the ways of wild animals like the wild ass which somehow lives in the most desolate of land—wilderness and salt lands? Can Job harness the great power of the wild ox and make the ox do his bidding and serve his purpose? These, too, are beyond Job's understanding and power.

What about that most majestic of creatures, the horse?

Do you give the horse its might?
  Do you clothe its neck with mane?
Do you make it leap like the locust?
  Its majestic snorting is terrible.
It paws violently, exults mightily;
  it goes out to meet the weapons.
It laughs at fear, and is not dismayed;
  it does not turn back from the sword.
Upon it rattle the quiver,
  the flashing spear, and the javelin.
With fierceness and rage it swallows the ground;
  it cannot stand still at the sound of the trumpet.
When the trumpet sounds, it says "Aha!"
  From a distance it smells the battle,
  the thunder of the captains, and the shouting. (39:19-25)

This is one of the most magnificent passages in the Book of Job. The poet makes us feel the barely restrained strength of the horse, whose power quivers through its body and whose neighing sends thrills of terror up and down our spines. The horse is eager for battle, impatient for the sound of the trumpet that announces the battle is about to be joined. The horse is scornful of danger, and its speed is so great that it appears to devour or swallow up the ground. Who is the source of this magnificent creature? Did Job create the horse or give it its power? No, God is the creator of the horse. How much greater, then, must God be as the source of such strength and beauty?

Does Job understand the skill of the hawk, the ability of the vulture to spot food from its station high in the sky? Could Job go fishing for a whale and hope to reel it in?

> Can you draw out Leviathan with a fishhook,
>> or press down its tongue with a cord?
> Can you put a rope in its nose,
>> or pierce its jaw with a hook?
> Will it make many supplications to you?
>> Will it speak soft words to you?
> Will it make a covenant with you
>> to be taken as your servant forever?
> Will you play with it as with a bird,
>> or will you put it on leash for your girls?
> Will traders bargain over it?
>> Will they divide it up among the merchants? (41:1-6)

The problems with the speeches of God begin here. First, to what exactly do these verses refer? The Hebrew word *Leviathan* is a term used in Near Eastern mythology of a primeval dragon believed to inhabit the seas. In creation God subdued this dragon and its havoc-making, chaos-causing powers. 41:1 does not, however, refer to this mythological creature but rather to some actual creature really inhabiting a body of water—the sea, a river, a swamp. (This explains the reference to fishing for it.) The second problem is that the description of Leviathan has been confused with that of another animal, Behemoth, whose description begins in 40:15. Behemoth is clearly an animal that can function on land, whereas Leviathan is a sea creature. The description of Leviathan, placed as it is in chapter 41, is out of place, interrupting the description of Behemoth. So it is better to read 41:1-6 as the climax of the first speech. This allows the poem on Behemoth to read smoothly from 40:15 to the end of God's second speech without interruption (the description of Behemoth continues in 41:12).

What, then is Leviathan? It is a sea creature which could not be pulled out of the sea by the ordinary means of fishing. It is a creature so enormous and powerful that the implements of fishing cause it no anxiety or fear. Its power is so great that it would never have to plead for mercy or beg for its life. Going after Leviathan is not like getting a pet to have around the house. And if, though impossible, Job *should* capture Leviathan, what would he do with it? It is so enormous that it would have to be divided among Job's associates, and it would have to be sold to several merchants, because one would not be able to handle it all. This description points to the largest of all earthly creatures, the whale. Job could not possibly hope to subdue Leviathan. Yet, Job has taken on God, Leviathan's creator.

The point of God's first speech is obvious. God is the creator of the earth and sea and heavens. God is the giver of life to all living things. God is the source of the power and strength of the horse and whale. Job cannot begin to comprehend these wonders of nature. Yet he has dared to challenge the creator of all these things. How could he possibly hope to understand God when he cannot understand the world God created?

God's Address to Job

God's questions cannot be answered. God knows it, Job knows it, we know it. There is a long silent pause during which God lets this point silently sink in. Then God addresses Job: "Is it for a man who disputes with the Almighty to be stubborn? Should he who argues with God answer back?" Job has had a moment to think about everything—the whole dialogue, his defense, God's overwhelming rhetorical questions. God puts it to him: Will you be stubborn? Will you continue to argue? Job had asked for an audience with God in order to question and be questioned. But is there anything for him to say? God has not answered Job's questions about how to reconcile human suffering with a world created by God. But there is now no point in pursuing them, so Job says:

> See, I am of small account; what shall I answer you?
>> I lay my hand on my mouth.
> I have spoken once, and I will not answer;
>> twice, but will proceed no further. (40:4-5)

Job poignantly describes his condition before God as carrying no weight. Since God has appeared in the midst of a raging thunderstorm, Job pictures himself being tossed about like a leaf. He puts his hand to his mouth as a sign of silent reverence and awe and also, perhaps, to keep himself from saying something he might later regret. Though he is now like a leaf tossed about in the wind, the gesture of silencing himself by putting his hand to his lips recalls the earlier time when he was more substantial—his friends once did that as a sign of honor to him (29:9). To emphasize his resolution not to say anything else, he uses the formula "spoken once . . . spoken twice" which means, I have said all there is to say. I have nothing more to say.

God's Second Speech

The storm renews itself, and God renews the interrogation of Job:

> Gird up your loins like a man;
>> I will question you, and you declare to me.
> Will you even put me in the wrong?
>> Will you condemn me that you may be justified?
> Have you an arm like God,
>> and can you thunder with a voice like his?
> Deck yourself with majesty and dignity;
>> clothe yourself with glory and splendor.
> Pour out the overflowings of your anger,
>> and look on all who are proud, and abase them.
> Look on all who are proud, and bring them low;
>> tread down the wicked where they stand.
> Hide them all in the dust together,
>> bind their faces in the world below.
> Then I will also acknowledge to you
>> that your own right hand can give you victory. (40:7-14)

Once again God commands Job to prepare to defend himself. This time, though, God finally deals directly with the question of whether or not there can be divine justice in a world where people suffer. Job has claimed that suffering like his—in the absence of any adequate explanation—proves that God is unjust. To justify himself is one thing, but to do it at God's expense is another. Can Job do the things that God can do? Is Job's arm like God's arm? If Job speaks will his voice sound like thunder and accomplish, by speaking alone, what he has said? Let Job do his best, put on his very best clothes, call up all his reserves of self-esteem. Can he by doing so humble the proud or bring down the wicked? If he unleashes the fury of his wrath, like God unleashes lightning bolts, will he thereby make the world more just? Can he do anything to punish the wicked and bring them to an ignominious end? When Job can exercise such moral authority, then he will have the right to criticize God's moral governance of the world.

This response, of course, avoids the real issue Job has raised. Job naturally cannot bring about justice in the world. He is a mortal and lacks both the power and the wisdom to be the final arbiter of justice on earth. God presumably has both power and wisdom, yet one or the other seems to have failed in Job's case. Job believes that there must be some adequate reason for God to allow his sufferings. He has asked God to appear so he could find out what that reason is. And God avoids the issue. Job has maintained his faith in God in spite of everything because he believes there is an explanation for his suffering. And God rewards him with unanswerable rhetorical questions.

The greatest *non sequitur* of all in God's speeches now occurs—the poem about the crocodile (40:15-24; 41:12-34).

> Look at Behemoth,
>> which I made just as I made you;
>> it eats grass like an ox.
> Its strength is in its loins,
>> and its power in the muscles of its belly.
> It makes its tail stiff like a cedar;
>> the sinews of its thighs are knit together.
> Its bones are tubes of bronze,
>> its limbs like bars of iron.

It is the first of the great acts of God—
>   only its Maker can approach it with the sword.
For the mountains yield food for it
>   where all the wild animals play.
Under the lotus plants it lies,
>   in the covert of the reeds and in the marsh.
The lotus trees cover it for shade;
>   the willows of the wadi surround it.
Even if the river is turbulent, it is not frightened;
>   it is confident though Jordan rushes against its mouth.
Can one take it with hooks
>   or pierce its nose with a snare? (40:15-24)

God praises the crocodile for its great strength which makes it superior to other animals, even other wild beasts, which the crocodile can easily crunch in its powerful jaws. The crocodile, thus, is the chief of all beasts. (Not even the lion could successfully attack a crocodile.) Nothing fazes the crocodile. Even if its habitat, the stream or river, floods it is not bothered. It is magisterially indifferent to everything.

Even human beings pose no serious threat. Human implements are useless against such a powerful creature. The most advanced weapons of human technology (iron and bronze) are as effective as straw or rotting wood. What good, then, will those older and cruder weapons, the sling and the club, be? If angered, the crocodile "makes the deep boil like a pot" through the thrashing of its powerful tail.

It counts iron as straw,
>   and bronze as rotten wood.
The arrow cannot make it flee;
>   slingstones, for it, are turned to chaff.
Clubs are counted as chaff;
>   it laughs at the rattle of javelins.
Its underparts are like sharp potsherds;
>   it spreads itself like a threshing sledge on the mire.
It makes the deep boil like a pot;
>   it makes the sea like a pot of ointment.
It leaves a shining wake behind it;
>   one would think the deep to be white-haired.

> On earth it has no equal,
>> a creature without fear.
> It surveys everything that is lofty;
>> it is king over all that are proud. (41:27-34)

God's speeches do not so much end on this note as peter out. It is as though the poet has lost interest in the argument with Job or has forgotten the point intended by the description of the crocodile. Whatever the reasons, God's speeches come to an end. Their overall thrust seems to be that Job will be able to understand God when he is able to understand God's ways in nature. Job will have the right to criticize God's governance of the world when he demonstrates the power to control and subdue the creation, especially its mightiest creatures. If this is the argument, then it is an example of the *ad hominem* fallacy—attacking the one who raised the questions rather than answering the questions themselves.

God's speeches, for whatever reason, come to an end. The fury of the storm has spent itself. There is at last a silence which indicates an end to the dialogue, not merely a pause. One thing remains to be done. Job, whose inexplicable sufferings have been the occasion of the dialogue, needs to close it out with some kind of response. No one else has anything left to say.

Job's Submission

Job breaks the silence with these final words:

> I know that you can do all things,
>> and that no purpose of yours can be thwarted.
> "Who is this that hides counsel without knowledge?"
> Therefore I have uttered what I did not understand,
>> things too wonderful for me, which I did not know.
> "Hear, and I will speak;
>> I will question you, and you declare to me."
> I had heard of you by the hearing of the ear,
>> but now my eye sees you;
>>> therefore I despise myself, and repent in dust and ashes.
> (42:2-6)

Job's final statement contains two quotations from earlier speeches (which are indicated in the REB by the formula, "You ask" or "You said"). Job has the final word and maintains his integrity to the very end. First, he admits the obvious truth (which he never questioned) that God can do all things. Then he (ironically) contrasts his ignorance with God's perfect abilities by quoting God's initial words to him. The ironic quotation is Job's way of saying, Do you really think I ever questioned your power? Do you really think I was not fully conscious of my ignorance of your ways? Do you really think that I wanted to obscure your purposes? No. I wanted, always, to discover the truth of your ways, precisely because I was so aware of my ignorance. Job then makes the implication of his quotation explicit. He knew that he was speaking about mysteries he did not fully understand. God's appearance has overwhelmed him with that truth and made him painfully conscious of it. But he knew it all along. What other point did his questions have if not to show that he wanted to replace ignorance with knowledge, incomprehension with understanding?

Job quotes God again, again ironically, since God does not intend these questions to be answered. But the quote is doubly ironic, since God's original statement was a direct allusion to Job's requests for God to appear and be questioned (13:22; 23:4-5). Job got his wish all right—God appeared. But it was not at all what Job thought it would be. He was the one who had to answer questions.

Then one final thought. Job's religion had been a religion of tradition. His piety had been the orthodox piety of the friends based on the wisdom of human experience. But Job has now encountered God face to face, and his worship will now be based on that encounter. He can no longer say the kinds of things he used to say about God. His suffering and his experience of God's presence make him skeptical of his (or anyone's) ability to say much that is true. So, he repents—not of any sin but of having said things he has not really understood, things too wonderful for him to know.

On the most superficial level, God's speeches out of the storm seem to be nothing but a clubbing of Job into submission. Job never really has a chance to answer God's questions—which are unanswerable in any case. Job's desire was to see God for the purpose of asking God the reasons for his suffering. And though God gives Job an opportunity to respond, Job recognizes that it is useless to say anything.

Is God, then, little more than a divine bully? Is God's purpose simply to beat Job into the ground for having questioned divine justice? God's speeches can be read that way. But they can also be read as an affirmation of Job. God addresses Job directly and in doing that shows that Job can be held responsible for his words and deeds. Job is a *person,* that is, capable of direct address. God challenges Job by his speeches. Job has dared to ask questions no one else has even thought of. He has penetrated to the very heart of his problem while the friends have seen only the surface. God is saying in effect, Job, you have dared to look deeper than anyone else. You have seen that your suffering does create a problem, namely why I allow it. You have been willing to voice these questions, and you have been honest enough to draw the conclusions the answers to these questions seem to imply. Your conclusion that I am unjust is wrong. I am the God of justice. But you were at least honest enough to say what you really believed. How far are you willing to go, Job? How much reality can you take? This is who I am. I am the one who called the world into being. I am the one who sustains it. I understand and control the mysteries of earth and sea and sky. I understand and control the mysteries of living things. The mighty animals of the wild, who will never be captured or tamed by mortals, are but a faint image of my power and glory. This is who I am, this is the one you have challenged. I am prepared to go with you as far as you want to go. Stand up with pride and dignity. Gird yourself for a testing the likes of which you cannot begin to comprehend. *I* will question *you.*

Job has gone as far as he needs to go with God and as far as he can go. His encounter with the living God causes his questions to melt away like the morning mist. Having met the living God, Job no longer desires to ask questions. He was wrong to think that he could understand the ways of God, and he repents of this error. The encounter with God has given Job a new dignity and a new standing as a human being. God meets Job in personal encounter and honors him by taking his challenge to appear seriously. Job is the one who has integrity in spite of the enormous forces working to make him compromise. Job exhibits the courage to be. In appearing to Job, God affirms this integrity and this courage.

Human Suffering and the Persistence of Questions

When confronted with shattering experiences that threaten us with meaninglessness, we have two basic options. We can believe that these things just happen and that there is no explanation for them and that we must bear them the best we can. Or we can believe there is some explanation that would at least intellectually satisfy us (if not existentially). Job and his friends never consider the first option. Their disagreement is not about *whether* there is an explanation but rather *what* the explanation is. The reason they do not give in to meaninglessness and despair is that they cling to their faith in a God who rules the universe. Modern day atheism (*a la* Thomas Hardy) was not really a live option for them.

They do disagree, however, over what the correct explanation is. For Job's friends the explanation is clear and simple. Suffering is a sign of sinfulness. If one suffers one is being punished for sin. The friends believe their doctrine is based on human experience. But, in fact, as the dialogue quickly demonstrates, it turns into an a priori dogma. The evidence from experience is on Job's side that he is innocent, that his suffering is undeserved. He was after all renowned for righteousness. Job's case presents his friends with a hard choice. They can admit the facts and give up their dogma, or they can deny the facts and cling to their dogma. To their discredit, they choose the latter alternative. Thus, Eliphaz in the third cycle of speeches accuses Job of the worst sins he can imagine. And "imagine" is completely accurate. Eliphaz's catalogue of Job's sins is completely fictional, a preposterous show which demonstrates the length to which otherwise honest people will go in order to defend their dogmas.

Job's belief is that there is an explanation but that the commonly accepted one of his friends is inadequate. Job, in other words, accepts the facts and rejects the dogma. He is innocent, yet he is suffering. If there is a God, then there must be some explanation for his suffering other than the traditional view of his friends.

Since Job never considers the possibility that there isn't a God, he is committed to searching for the alternative explanations. One possibility is that God is malevolent, God is unjust, God desires Job's destruction—not for any sin of Job's but to satisfy God's own ill-will. In some of Job's more despairing moments he actually charges God with injustice and ill-will. But this possibility is not really characteristic of Job's thought. He pleads with God like a child with a parent, he constantly appeals to God to appear and explain his suffering. If Job really believed God was malevolent, he would not do that. He would try to avoid God's notice altogether rather than calling attention to himself.

Job really believes that God will be fair and will exonerate him. So Job considers another possibility—an arbitrator to listen to his case and judge between him and God. But this idea, he realizes, is foolish—who could make God conform to the arbitrator's judgment? Furthermore, Job is acutely aware that his time is short and that unless the arbitrator appears quickly, he will be dead and beyond vindication. Or will he? If his story were written in a book—or better yet, engraved on stone—he might be vindicated in the eyes of future generations even after his death. Or, better still, if there were only a living witness to proclaim him innocent. In a flash of insight, the implications of which the poet does not fully understand, Job sees his witness, *the Last,* standing on earth vindicating him. This living vindicator is none other than God.

Job therefore believes God will be fair and will exonerate him sometime, somehow, somewhere. Job believes there is a morally justifiable reason why God would allow him to suffer. Job's problem is that God is absent. He cannot, therefore, ask God what this reason is. But whether or not God appears, Job will not compromise his integrity by admitting to sins he did not commit. If that means rejection by his friends and further alienation from God, so be it. He has lived a life of integrity to this point, and he will not change now.

Job was right to believe God would exonerate him. When the storm bursts upon Job and his friends, God addresses Job as a person, as one to be held responsible for word and deed. Job has, of course, said wild things that need to be corrected. But at least he has spoken the truth as he knows it, unlike the friends who think they defend God when they twist the truth they know. Because of his integrity, Job can stand in the presence of God.

The poet has finished the drama. What does it show us about suffering in a world created by God? The first conclusion is a negative one: it is *not* true that suffering is always the punishment for sins. The facts of human existence are against it. Too often, the wicked prosper and the righteous suffer. Look at Job. Renowned for his righteousness, he loses everything. No one is convinced by the friends' desperate attempts to paint him as a blackguard. He is innocent, he suffers, and that creates a problem for one who believes and trusts in God. Job contends for this point throughout the speeches, and Job speaks for the poet.

Second, in spite of the suffering of the innocent, God is still just. This is the point of God's appearing and addressing Job in the storm—to defend the divine justice and correct Job's error of attributing injustice to God. This second point has the corollary that there *is* some explanation of suffering, because God's justice can only be maintained if there is some morally sufficient reason why God allows it. Again, Job insists all along that there must be some reason which justifies his suffering. His appeals for God to appear and answer his questions only make sense if there are answers. So, as a corollary of God's justice, we must assume there is an explanation.

But, third, the poet doesn't know what that explanation is. God doesn't answer Job's questions. Job's suffering remains unexplained. God's righteousness and justice, on the one hand, and human suffering, on the other, together make up the terms of an unfathomable mystery. Job realizes, as with irony he quotes God while submitting, that his questions have not been answered and will not be. There is almost a wistfulness about Job's answer to God at the last. He has gone through so much, explored every possibility to explain his suffering, been finally granted his audience with God—yet still no answers to his questions.

But finally, perhaps, the poet is saying that Job transcends the desire for intellectual satisfaction. The heat of direct, existential encounter with God melts Job's questions like ice cream on a sidewalk in Biloxi in July. Job has seen God, and God has become a living presence in Job's life. How important can those questions be?

In the heat of reading the book of Job, I believe we are satisfied with the way it ends. The poet ends the drama at the appropriate place. God has spoken, Job has submitted, this encounter invests Job with a new honor and dignity, the curtain falls, the play is over. Aesthetically we are satisfied. But philosophically questions nag at the back of our minds. Is there an explanation of Job's suffering that is consistent with God's goodness and power? If there is such an explanation, how could we come to know it? Why doesn't God simply reveal it to us? Can we discover an explanation by means of reason? Is it impious to ask for intellectual satisfaction?

The poet may have never asked these questions. To us, though, they are important because we are philosophical in a way the Hebrew people never were. Our cultural traditions include the Greek as well as the Hebrew. That means we are concerned with reason and logic. Hence, the questions Job raised will not go quietly away. In our reflective moments they demand an answer of some sort.

The Book of Job itself offers some justification for proceeding with philosophical concerns. Above all else, Job desires an explanation of his suffering. His friends offer one which does answer the question but which, unfortunately, fails because it is based on a false premise. So Job rejects one possible (and widely accepted) solution. Either there is no solution (Hardy was right, it is "crass casualty" and "dicing time") or there is an explanation which has not yet been articulated. Job rejects the first disjunct because, if true, certain monstrous consequences would follow. The universe would no longer be intelligible to him. Its existence and processes would be sheer chance occurrences. At any moment it might collapse back into the chaos from which it came. Job's undeserved suffering would simply be a threatening reminder that reality is a chaos not a cosmos. Job cannot accept this half of the disjunction with the irrationality it entails. Thus, he must affirm the second solution—there *is* an explanation but unfortunately no one has yet discovered what it is.

Why does Job cling so desperately to his belief that his suffering is intelligible and that the universe itself is intelligible? The answer is that Job believes in God and believes that God is ultimately good, wise, just, powerful, and caring. God is the sovereign over

Chapter 7

Suffering and a God of Love

All of us suffer from time to time. Much of our pain is trivial—a toothache, a headache, a pain in the back (though at the time it may not *seem* trivial). We go to the dentist, and he extracts the tooth. We go to the doctor, and she prescribes medicine. Very seldom does this ordinary, every-day suffering raise questions about the goodness or power of God. We suffer it, take care of it, and forget it.

But there are times when suffering is not so easily dismissed. We see documentaries about Nazi death camps, we read about genocide in Cambodia, we hear news reports of Christian troops systematically slaughtering Arab civilians in Beirut. Daily, it seems, our news media confront us with such stories. But suffering need not make the headlines to cause us to question God. We know a beautiful child who dies of leukemia after a long and painful struggle. Her parents look on helplessly while doctors try everything they can but to no avail. Why did God not do something to save this child, so beautiful and full of promise? We see a friend whose emotional instability causes him to lose his job and threatens the well-being of his family who depend on him economically. Why didn't God heal that emotional wound?

When we are personally touched by such suffering or witness it in the lives of others, we cannot help but ask why a God of goodness and love allows such things to happen. The question why is really two questions. It is an existential question: How am I going to cope? And it is also an intellectual question: How can there be such suffering in a world created by a good and loving God? The Book of Job offers an answer to the first question: the presence of God. God appears finally, addresses Job directly, and affirms Job's integrity. This affirmation gives Job strength and restores the meaning and sense of purpose he had lost. The universe is not, after all, an amoral chaos without moral purpose. God cares enough for Job to confront him personally and challenges him to go as far as he can in understanding God and God's creation and the place of persons in that creation. God's appearance is, ultimately, an act of love. But the intellectual questions are not answered. If we are to answer them, we must venture beyond the Book of Job.

The Problem of Suffering

We may state the problem of suffering this way. God is perfectly good and, therefore, would *want* to eliminate suffering because suffering is bad. God is perfectly powerful and, therefore, *could* eliminate suffering. God's goodness provides the motive, God's omnipotence the power. Yet suffering exists. Formally, the problem is that we want to affirm three propositions which cannot all, apparently, be true:

(1) God is perfectly good.
(2) God is all-powerful.
(3) Suffering exists.

We want to affirm the first two because we intuitively feel they are necessary attributes of God. We want to affirm the third because of the facts of human existence. At least one of these propositions, it seems, must be false. Which one?

Must we affirm proposition three, "Suffering exists"? I said that the facts require us to affirm it. The problem disappears, however, if suffering is not really real. This is the view of some persons, like Christian Scientists. Suffering is not really real but rather an illusion based on our misapprehension of reality. We cannot explore the arguments that might be used to support such a claim. Suffice it to say that they would have to be exceedingly powerful, cogent, and persuasive arguments to convince most of us. Suffering is too real to most of us, so the burden of proof lies with the one who denies its reality.

Perhaps, then, God is not perfectly powerful. Denying proposition two also solves the problem. This is the solution Rabbi Harold Kushner proposed in his best-selling book *When Bad Things Happen to Good People.* Bad things happen to good people like Job because God cannot stop them from happening. There are limits to God's power. Though God wants to arrest suffering, God can't.

If our only alternatives are to reject one of the three propositions above, then to me this is the best alternative. I agree with Rabbi Kushner, in other words, that *if* these three propositions are in fact incompatible, this is the one we should deny. Rabbi Kushner's denial of God's omnipotence is placed in the context of a discussion of petitionary prayer. He relates the story of how a stranger called him late one night and requested that he pray for his mother who was to have a serious operation the next day. Rabbi Kushner makes the following comment:

> Praying for a person's health, for a favorable outcome of an operation, has implications that ought to disturb a thoughtful person. If prayer worked the way many people think it does, no one would ever die, because no prayer is ever offered more sincerely than the prayer for life, for health and recovery from illness, for ourselves and for those we love.

> If we believe in God, but we do not hold God responsible for life's tragedies, if we believe that God wants justice and fairness *but cannot always arrange for them,* what are we doing when we pray to God for a favorable outcome to a crisis in our life?

> *Do I—and does the man who called me—really believe in a God who has the power to cure malignancies and influence the outcome of surgery,* and will do that only if the right person recites the right words in the right language? And will God let a person die because a stranger, praying on her behalf, got some of the words wrong? Who among us could respect or worship a God whose implicit message was "I could have made your mother healthy again, but you didn't plead and grovel enough"?[1]

---

1. Harold Kushner, *When Bad Things Happen to Good People* (New York: Avon Books, 1983)113–114. Italics added.

There are two ideas here I want to consider. The first concerns God's power. The italicized passages clearly indicate that Rabbi Kushner believes God's power is limited. God cannot always "arrange for" justice and fairness. (Does this mean that God sometimes can?) The force of the rhetorical question in the second passage is clearly to deny that God has the power to do things like cure malignancies or ensure the success of operations. Later in the same chapter Kushner writes:

> God does not want you to be sick or crippled. He didn't make you have this problem, and He doesn't want you to go on having it, but he can't make it go away. That is something which is too hard even for God.[2]

So, God didn't want the calamities that befell Job to happen to him. But God couldn't do anything about it. God is not omnipotent.

This solves the problem of suffering. The contradiction between our three propositions disappears because we have eliminated one of them. Rabbi Kushner makes a powerful and appealing case for this solution. But we need to ask: Is it really religiously sound? Does it do justice to religious belief and practice? At this point we need to examine the second important idea expressed in the first passage—Kushner's concept of petitionary prayer (that is, prayer in which we petition God for something, such as recovery from illness or a safe journey). This kind of prayer, according to Rabbi Kushner, is an attempt to manipulate God. At least, that is what many people seem to believe. If only the right person recites the right words in the right way, then God will automatically grant the request. This sort of attitude is unworthy of us, and we ought not pray in this way. However, prayer is something we ought to do, according to Kushner. Why? Not because God is going to answer our prayers but rather because we can derive strength from it. Prayer puts us in contact with people, with those who pray with us and for us. It also puts us in contact with God. What we should pray for is not that the problem will go away but that we will find the strength to deal with it. This is a prayer God can answer.

---

2. Ibid., 129.

Rabbi Kushner is right in what he affirms, but wrong in what he denies. He affirms that prayer puts us in contact with people and God and that we derive strength from such contact. All of this is true. But he denies that God has the power to do anything about the causes of our suffering. On this point I believe he is wrong. For one thing, the Bible itself (especially the Psalms) is full of prayers for deliverance in time of trouble. They are, for the most part, not attempts to manipulate God but rather sincere expressions of desire for deliverance and faith that God *can* deliver. It is a normal, healthy human reaction to want to be delivered from a threatening crisis, and the expression of this desire in prayer (in and of itself) is not bad. The point is that petitionary prayer is a normal part of religious experience. And if we admit this, then we must admit something else as well, namely, the implication of such prayer is that God has the power to grant our petition. The logic of petitionary prayer is that God can do what we ask. To deny God's power has, I believe, profound negative consequences for religious practice. If God is not perfectly powerful, God is reduced essentially to the same status as the parents of the child dying of leukemia. They could do nothing to alleviate their child's suffering. The doctors were, in fact, in a better position than God because they at least could do something. Even to believe in a very, very powerful but nevertheless limited, finite God would not be sufficient for the actual practice of religion. If God's power is not perfect, how can we be sure that God is dependable? How can we be sure that there is no other power greater than God and that that other power will not overrule God? In short, religious devotion and practice seem to demand a God who is all powerful.

What, then, about the first proposition, "God is perfectly good"? Job entertains the idea that God may be malevolent, but not for long. His better religious instincts lead him away from that possibility. It would be monstrous to worship an omnipotent being whose goodness could not be counted on in every circumstance. It would be better to deny the existence of God altogether than to assert the existence of an all-powerful but morally imperfect God. Religious practice and devotion demand, with even greater insistence than the case of God's power, a God who is all good.

The dilemma we are struggling with arises because we have assumed these three propositions are mutually inconsistent. We have tried to resolve the dilemma by "grasping it by the horns"—by denying one or the other of the propositions which together constitute the dilemma. This process leads to unwelcome consequences so that we become impaled on the dilemma's horns. We ought, then, to consider the other way of dealing with a dilemma—going between the horns, showing that these propositions are not mutually inconsistent after all.

This is the approach adopted by most theistic thinkers. The assumption that allows us to go between the horns is the assumption that there is a morally sufficient reason for God to allow suffering. Such a reason, since *morally* sufficient, would not offend against God's goodness. And such a reason, since morally *sufficient*, would not detract from God's power. Furthermore, most theists approach this problem by distinguishing between two different causes of suffering—human choice and the natural order. We will adopt this distinction and examine first suffering caused by deliberate human choice.

Human Freedom and Moral Evil

Suffering caused by deliberate human choice is what theologians and philosophers call "moral evil." Job experienced this kind of evil when his friends accused him of sin and refused to allow that he might be innocent. They deliberately chose to ignore his arguments and their own knowledge of him and accused him anyhow, knowing he would be hurt by their words. Since Job *was* innocent, his suffering at the hands of his friends was unnecessary and only increased his burden of alienation. Unnecessary and useless suffering is surely an evil which an all good God would want to eliminate and an all powerful God could eliminate. Yet, God did nothing.

What should God have done? Should God have struck Eliphaz dumb when he began to accuse Job? Should God have miraculously altered the sound waves Eliphaz's voice made so that they produced pleasant or innocuous meanings in Job's ears? Perhaps God should have simply made Eliphaz more sensitive to the feelings of others, so he would have known better than to say those hurtful things to Job. Surely, God could have done any of those things. But doing them would be to interfere with Eliphaz's free choice. Eliphaz says what he does to Job because of the person he is, and he is the person he is largely because of the choices he has made. Do we want God to interfere with Eliphaz's freedom to choose?

Many people, especially when they consider the results of free choice in the case of a Hitler or a Stalin, are inclined to say yes— it *would* be better for God to interfere with human freedom, if such interference would eliminate suffering caused by deliberate human choice. Or, better yet, why did God not create us so that we would always do the right thing? Some philosophers have argued that God could have created human beings with free choice who nevertheless would always choose the good.

These are powerful arguments, and for many people they will be convincing. Yet, there are questions we need to ask. For example, what does it mean to say that we could be granted free choice but be unable to choose anything but the good? The problem with this argument is that it vacates the concept of human goodness of its ordinary meaning. How can I be called good if there was never any choice at all for me to be bad? For human beings, at least, the concept of goodness implies the possibility of being bad. Unless this possibility of evil is so, we are not really considering human beings but some other kind of being.

Perhaps, then, God should not have created *human* beings but rather beings resembling us who could only choose the good. If free choice is necessary to being human, then God should not have made human beings. This reply, however, implies that such beings would be better than mere human beings, because God by nature would always do what is the best. But would such creatures be better than human beings? They are capable only of good while human beings are capable of either good or evil, depending on their choices. Intuitively, we feel that an act of goodness chosen when the agent could have chosen evil is better (morally) than the same act done when there was no possibility of doing anything else. The reason is that the goodness of the human agent is a goodness created by the agent, and we can blame him or hold her responsible for the act. The goodness of an agent who can only do the good does not involve his or her goodness. She or he doesn't choose between possible alternatives. The choice is made because it cannot be otherwise. Perhaps it would have been better for God to create beings who could only do the good. But the burden of proof seems to lie with the one who makes this assertion. Intuitively, we feel that human goodness, because it is chosen, is better than a programmed goodness which is automatic.

If, therefore, it was better for God to create human beings— beings capable of choosing between good and evil—it follows that some of them may choose evil instead of good. And if they choose evil, suffering may occur. Because they are human, God allows them to choose evil. Constant interference by God when we choose the wrong would violate our humanness. And it is better to have human beings who can choose either good or evil than to have other beings who can choose only the good. Therefore, there is a morally sufficient reason for this kind of suffering.

A Contingent World and Physical Evil

The concept of the human offers a solution to the problem of suffering when that arises from the deliberate human choice of evil. But even if we accept the foregoing argument, it does not explain suffering which results from the natural order rather than human choice. Tornadoes, for example, suddenly strike a city destroying life and property. A beautiful child dies a prolonged and painful death from leukemia. Job contracts a disfiguring skin disease which leaves his friends speechless when they first come to comfort him. None of these examples can be explained in terms of human choice. Instead, they all result from the natural ordering of the world. God created the natural world the way it is. We had nothing to do with it. Therefore, God must be held responsible for this kind of suffering.

Let us restate the argument more explicitly. God created the world. The world as created necessarily produces suffering in the form of physical pain and death for its sentient creatures. As creator, God could foresee that this world would produce these consequences. Since God is all-powerful, God could have created a world in which the physical order never posed a threat to the well-being of its inhabitants. Thus, God must be held responsible for this kind of suffering. And if so, God is not perfectly good. And if not perfectly good, then not God (as traditionally conceived). It follows, then, that unless there is a morally sufficient reason for God to create a physical world where suffering will occur, God (so conceived) does not exist.

As in the case of moral suffering, we need to ask what it is exactly we want God to do. For example, if I am unable to swim and I fall into deep water, should God change the water into air, miraculously grant me ad hoc the ability to swim, miraculously lengthen my legs so they will reach the bottom (like one of the five Chinese brothers)? On the crudest level, this criticism seems to call for God's constant interference in the natural order. But we ought not to take this criticism on the lowest level of interpretation. Instead, the real point is that God should not have created a universe where dangerous, hurtful things can happen. The universe should have been created free of the possibility that its sentient creatures could suffer. In other words, this criticism really proposes a hypothetical universe, one which doesn't exist but which we can conceive of existing.

What would such a universe be like? Since it is hypothetical, it could be anything we can conceive. But also, since it is hypothetical, it will probably resemble our real universe in many ways. Science fiction writers create alternate worlds which, however different from our own, nevertheless are also very much like our own. Furthermore, we ought to remember that our world as constituted contains not only hurtful elements but also elements such as beauty and health which produce joy, happiness, and well-being, so that at times we can honestly say, "It's good to be alive." It is reasonable to assume that the critic proposing a hypothetical, better universe would want this universe to contain these elements of joy, happiness, and well-being without the elements which produce evil and suffering. In short, the hypothetical world God should have made and could have made would be very similar to the one we now live in but different in that none of its elements could produce suffering.

If this world is similar to ours, we would probably have to admit into it some pain or at least some discomfort. We would, for example, probably allow for hunger while denying that anyone could starve. Hunger pangs are not unpleasant when we know that there is no question of having them satisfied. We would probably allow winter to be cold—but not so cold that one could ever freeze to death. And the cold would be regulated so that there would be lovely snowfalls and frozen ponds for ice-skating. We would probably want summer to be hot—going to the beach is not much fun without a hot sun overhead—but not so hot that there would be droughts or heat strokes. A certain amount of discomfort is allowable as long as there is no possibility of its getting out of hand and posing a real threat. Rain would always fall at the right time and in the right amounts on the right places, but there would never be thunderstorms or floods which caused destruction or death. (There might be thunderstorms and floods, but they could never pose a threat to our well-being.) Micro-organisms would never induce disease, only health. Would death be possible? Probably death should be ruled out because even if it were painless, it would produce suffering in the living through their sense of loss.

In short, the world we say God should have created is a world with all the pleasant, good features and none of the negative ones of our present world. Such a concept appears plausible. The problem is that it is not. In reality, it is incoherent. Our concept of "world" or "universe" is based on our experience of the only world we know—the one we live in. And our world, as revealed through the natural sciences, is one of interlocking unity. The very conditions that make possible the gentle spring rains which water our crops also make possible the violent summer storms which destroy life and property. The regularities which make for the life-sustaining production of blood cells also make possible death-dealing cancers like leukemia. When we talk about a world that contains only the pleasant features of our present world and omits the unpleasant features, we know not of what we talk. It is even unclear whether or not we should call such a place "world" or "universe" because it violates a fundamental characteristic of the only world we know—the interlocking physical unity of our present universe.

Of course, this argument does not prove that there might not be such a world. It only proves that we do not know what it is we are talking about when we talk about it. It is always possible, therefore, that God could have and should have created such a world. With our present knowledge we cannot know if such a world might have existed. So, a better response to this criticism would be to show that our present world, as created, fulfills a morally justifiable purpose in a way no other world could have.

For us, the most significant fact about our world is that human beings have evolved in it. One essential feature of being human is the capacity for intelligence; another, as we have already seen, is free choice. Human intelligence makes it possible for us to deliberate rationally. And rational deliberation makes free choice possible. We are, therefore, essentially moral creatures, and all other human characteristics derive from these two. These capacities make language possible—the ability to communicate ideas and express feelings in some abstract way. Language makes possible the formation of society on a widespread basis. Societies inevitably take on political organization, support nonessential activities like art and literature, and provide for the common well-being. All of these traits of humanness come together in what we call culture or civilization.

It is difficult to see how any of these defining characteristics could have developed in a perfect world. We develop our intelligence by facing a problem which will not resolve itself. Choice becomes possible when the world presents us with alternatives which our intelligence discerns and evaluates. It seems that a contingent world—one which is unpredictable and threatening to a degree—is a necessary element in producing human beings. A perfect world with no threatening challenges would never provide the stimulus to develop intelligence or exercise choice. If there is no need to exercise choice, there can be no moral development, no sense that some things are right and some are wrong and that one ought to choose the right and shun the wrong. In a perfect world, a noncontingent world, there is no need for Job's integrity because there would never arise the ambiguous circumstances which would call it into question.

But is this game worth the candle? Is the producing of persons worth the creation of a contingent world in which suffering can at times be unbearable? Is this a morally sufficient reason? Perhaps we are being guilty here of arrogant anthropocentrism. Why should the characteristics essential to being human be the highest values? Why should human existence be more highly valued than, say, the existence of an amoeba? If the amoeba could, it might very well evaluate things differently. But that is the problem. As far as we know the amoeba cannot put the highest value on its existence because, as far as we know, it lacks developed intelligence and the ability to choose. And if an amoeba were granted intelligence and choice, what would it choose? Simple, unconscious amoeba-existence, or self-conscious, intelligent, free existence? Since this is an impossible hypothesis, we cannot answer the question. But intuitively, I believe most of us would say the latter.

Perhaps, though, this is an unfair comparison. We ought to compare human existence with that of the higher mammals rather than that of the lowly amoeba. Why, then, value human existence over, say, porpoises or dolphins? The answer is that what we value is intelligence and the ability to freely choose. If we ever encounter these qualities in creatures which are not biologically human, then they should be valued as morally equivalent to human beings.

There may be higher values in the universe than those we experience as essential to our own natures. But there are none that we know now, and it is difficult to conceive of what could be valued more highly than intelligence and free choice in a physical universe. And for such values to exist, a contingent world where suffering may occur seems necessary.

So, God does not send physical suffering deliberately to us, to punish us or for any other reason. God allows physical suffering to occur as a result of the natural processes of the world, because only in such a world is it possible to produce persons. If true, this would explain the physical sufferings of Job.

But is this explanation the true one? Each of us must decide that question. It attracts me because suffering seems somehow connected with our humanity. Faced with suffering, we can achieve levels of human development we would otherwise miss— of courage, honesty, self-sacrifice, intelligence, and integrity. Job was certainly changed by his experience. He is, ironically, wiser at the end than at the beginning; ironically, because his new wisdom was possible only by rejecting the old wisdom. Suffering has the potential to be redemptive.

But the obverse is also true: suffering is potentially destructive. If suffering can make us more human, it can make us less human too. Suffering can dehumanize us. For every Anne Frank who can say, "In spite of everything I still believe that people are really good at heart," there are many whose suffering seems pointless, meaningless, without any redeeming significance. Probably no century in human history has equalled ours in the brutality and senselessness of human suffering. And so, we cannot know whether the possibility that suffering can make us more human is a morally sufficient reason for God to allow it. If one accepts such an explanation, it will probably be that the explanation fits in with a whole universe of other beliefs and is not merely accepted in isolation. I believe in God, and I believe that God is loving and caring for all the creation including the human creation, so I believe there is an explanation for the suffering we experience consistent with God's existence. But I don't know that this explanation is the correct one. Job never learned the answer to the question of why he suffered. We don't learn it either. One who believes in God will have to believe that there is such a reason. That is part of what having faith in God means. And one who has such faith can confidently explore possible answers. But such faith—if it is a wise faith—will also be skeptical of most answers, even as Job was skeptical of his friends'. The example of Job teaches us that the best response when confronted by suffering—our own or others'—is to be honest, to hold on to our moral and intellectual integrity, to do what we *can* to alleviate the suffering, and to wait for a word from God.